BLUE ANGELS AND WHALES

BLUE ANGELS AND WHALES

A RECORD OF
PERSONAL EXPERIENCES
BELOW AND ABOVE WATER

BY

ROBERT GIBBINGS

WITH ILLUSTRATIONS BY THE AUTHOR

LONDON : J. M. DENT AND SONS LTD.

To ELISABETH

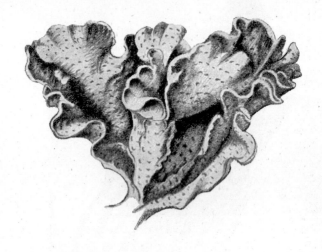

CONTENTS

CHAPTER I

TAHITI

'You seem to be in a bit of a hurry,' said the American consul at Tahiti, one day, as, a little out of breath, I stepped from my canoe and pulled it up on the edge of the lagoon.

'I was wondering,' said I, 'if sharks often attack canoes.'

'Man alive,' he answered laughing, 'they never even attack swimmers in here. There's fellows fishing and playing about in the lagoon all day long, and never a one has ever been touched. But try a dip outside the reef and it's a mighty different story. There they'll have you before you kick twice. In here, why, you're as safe as in your own bath.'

'What about that atoll up in the Paumotus,' I inquired, 'where the diving was held up for a fortnight?'

'Tiger shark,' he said, 'got in the lagoon by accident. Shouldn't have been there at all. You won't get them in here. I tell you, you can swim all over this lagoon, and if you 're minded to shut your eyes and drop asleep for a while and a shark happens to come along, he 'll just steal away without as much as a flip of his tail, for fear of waking you.'

This was comforting to a newcomer to the islands. Truth to tell, I 'd had a bit of scare when, looking over the edge of my canoe, I 'd seen the grey snout of a ten-foot shark who was squinting up at me with little tenderness in his eye. I had been floating over the lagoon watching the multitudes of brightly coloured fish swimming in and out of the almost unbelievably varied coral formations, and I had just about come to the momentous conclusion that, henceforth in life, a study of the reef and its associated fauna must be my chief concern, when that sudden apparition from the depths created, not only a vacuum in my stomach but a quick revision of my vocational intentions.

'What you 've really got to be careful of,' said my companion, 'is the stonefish; ugly damn brute, the dead spit of a stone on the bottom. If you step on him you 'll know all about it for an hour or two, and then,' he added as an afterthought, 'you 'll know nothing more about anything else ever again.'

I had heard yarns about these creatures before. They were said to be repulsive in appearance, their blotched and warty skin hardly distinguishable from a weed-encrusted stone. Thirteen spines, each with a pair of poison glands at its base, stood along their backs. Fishermen whose hands had accidentally touched the spines were said to have been driven delirious by the pain, even trying to amputate their own wounded limb. Men who had trodden on the fishes' back and received the full charge of poison into their feet were known to have died in agony.

'Wear strong leather shoes and watch where you step,' added my companion, 'and you 're in no greater danger than crossing Fifth Avenue.' Then, as we moved along to the club, he emphasized that no shark had ever touched a human being in the Tahiti lagoon, and no coco-nut had ever fallen on a man's head. I hoped that I wouldn't be the one to break a record.

Captain Muldoon was at the club.

> 'Micky Muldoon from Mullingar,
> With limbs as thick as a mainsail spar,
> Not an inch of his skin without a scar,
> And his blood as thick as Stockholm tar,'

as a local poet had written of him.

'What in hell d' ye want, lookin' at reef fish?' he asked. 'Couldn't ye see the finest salmon in the world in Ireland?'

'Looking for mermaids,' suggested Eriksen the Dane. Ever romantic, yet never in love, this big, blond, bald-headed man was rarely seen without one of the little white tiare blossoms behind his left ear. In Tahiti, a flower behind the left ear means 'I want a lover.' If worn behind the right ear it means 'I 've got one.'

'Looking for trouble,' said Munro from New Zealand. Like Rupert Brooke and many another unwary traveller he had suffered from coral poisoning. Ten weeks he had lain in bed with both legs and part of his body covered in sores, all through a scratch incurred while bathing. 'If you get a cut, keep out of the water until it's healed,' he told me. 'A coral cut will never heal if you let the salt water at it.'

The conversation reverted to sharks. Eriksen took from his pocket a wooden shark hook, some seven inches in length. 'Picked it up on a junk stall in the market, this morning,' he said. 'It's ironwood, one of the real old-timers. In those days a native would scrape away the soil at the root of a tree, bend the rootlet to the right shape, pin it down, cover it up, and let it go on growing for a number of years. Then he would scrape away the earth again, cut out the root, trim off the outer soft wood, and inside he'd have a hard inner core of just the shape he wanted. No need for a barb if he got the curve right, but a tip of bone was a help; some whisper a tip of human bone, but that was probably on another island. It's the same wood they use to-day for fish spears, hard as iron and sinks in water.'

Our party grew as other members of the club dropped in, but the talk about sharks continued. One said that there were still people in Tahiti who believed that the chiefs of ancient times had, after death, taken the form of sharks, and that they could still be seen frequenting particular parts of the lagoon. Another said that such a belief was almost certainly connected with a legend in the Marquesas Islands. This told how, one day, two large sharks arrived in one of the bays. The priest of the district, recognizing the visitors as gods, sent a servant to feed them. But one of the sharks was not content with the food offered: it claimed human flesh. The priest, being informed of this, decided that the servant's daughter, a virgin of marriageable years, should be the victim. Accordingly, with much lamentation, the servant led his own child to the water's edge. The shark was waiting, and seemed in no way averse to the choice; in fact, it swallowed the girl whole. Then it turned tail and swam to the island of Eiao, where it put her ashore. Meanwhile the other shark, in a similar way, had brought a youth from another island and put him ashore also. As seems inevitable the two young people then got married. It would not be difficult to imagine, suggested the speaker, that from such a union a line of chiefs might arise who could assume the form of sharks at will.

Then the interest turned from the supernatural powers of chiefs to the eccentricities of evil spirits. Authentic personal experiences were told of pebble throwing by unseen hands, pebbles which were unlike any to be found on the island, and there were tales of walls being spattered with fresh human blood—it had been analysed—though no one on the island had been hurt. Then legend took precedence again and Eriksen told a tale from Tonga. 'There was once a demon who lived in a house on the edge of the lagoon,' he said, 'and every bit of the framework of the house was built of beautiful young men and young women who had been captured and bound into the building. Only one "beam" was missing, that for the ridge-pole. And for this ridge-pole the demon was waiting until he should find a girl more beautiful than any that he had already made captive. From village to village and from island to island he hunted. Days, weeks, and months he spent in searching, until at last he found such a one as his eyes desired. Then he returned with her to his house, in triumph. And such was the beauty of this girl that even those who were already imprisoned in the fabric smiled with admiration when they saw her. But she herself could only weep and lament, knowing the fate that awaited her. The tears ran down her face and dropped on to her breasts, shining there like large lustrous pearls, and her plaintive sighs were like the murmuring of *Lupe*, the wild pigeon. Suddenly, moved by her tears as well as by her beauty, the demon changed his mind. Instead of fastening the thongs which would bind her for ever he took her by the hand and led her to the shore. There he begged that she would kill him. Again and again he demanded this of her. But he was so repulsive that she could only cower away. She could not bring herself to touch him even with a knife. Seeing her aversion he plunged into the water, intending to drown himself, and for a while his body was lost to view in the waves. Then to the surprise of all, there came from the sea, in his place, a magnificent young man, the demon transformed. He set free all his captives, married the girl, and all was peace and happiness.'

'Which shows the power of love,' said Muldoon. And, with that, the party broke up.

CHAPTER II

THE REEF

I HAD journeyed to the Pacific expecting to find interest in a strange and picturesque people. I had hoped to delight in all the luxuriance of the tropics: hedges of hibiscus, avenues of frangipane and flamboyant trees, groves of mangoes, guavas, and bananas; and I had looked forward with not a little pleasurable anticipation to native feasts, moonlight dances, and the other romantic incidents that are usually associated with the islands. But from that first day when I floated over those coral gardens I knew that henceforth my allegiance must be to Neptune. I forgot, entirely, those other deities Venus and Dionysus, who held a more general sway in the islands.

There were parties, of course. Yes, plenty of them; and I'm not suggesting that I turned in to a lonely cot when the moon was rising over the banana groves and the drums were beating out a rhythm for swaying hips. Neither do I pretend that I refused all invitations to picnic in the valleys, or bathe in the streams that cascaded down from the hills. But these entertainments became of less and less interest, and eventually were no more than occasional relaxations from the new and absorbing subject of inquiry to which I had fallen victim.

At the time I knew absolutely nothing about these fish, except that they were superlatively beautiful. They appeared to me more gorgeous than anything I had ever seen before, their shapes, their markings, and their colours seeming to vie with each other as to which could be the most bizarre. So every morning while the surface of the lagoon was still unruffled, and every evening when the trade wind had died down, I would spend hour after hour drifting in the canoe, watching with amazement this multicoloured under-water panorama which unfolded below me.

The longer I stayed on the island the more enamoured I became of 'the reef.' But it did not take me many days to realize that the inhabitants of this coral world viewed any shadow overhead with suspicion and that by approaching them from a canoe I was missing a great many of the shyer individuals. I then tried to meet them on more equal terms by immersing myself chin-deep in the water. This was successful. Provided I remained still, the fish would appear from their hiding-places, and, crowding round me, would pick at the chewed-up fragments of coco-nut which I spat into the water.

After a few weeks I made friends with an Irishman called Carney. He had a Japanese friend called Kono, and a Chinese maid of all work called Kitchee. Kono and Carney would go fishing at night, and in the morning Kitchee would bring me any specimens that were not wanted in the kitchen. Sometimes I would take Carney's place in the stern of the canoe, paddling slowly while Kono, standing in the bow with a foot on either gunwale and holding a torch in one hand, would strike now right, now left, at the fish that came towards us, attracted by the light. Kono had been born and bred in the islands. His skin was as dark as that of a Polynesian. He wore only the Tahitian *pareu* about his loins. He balanced with ease in the prow of this, to me most precarious, craft, silhouetted against the light of his own torch. His spear was multiple-pointed, each of the half-dozen or more prongs having a barb on its inner side. The prongs were bent slightly outwards from their junction with the spear-handle so that it was a cone of many points rather than a single one which struck at the fish. For that reason far more fish were caught between the prongs, with scarcely a scale damaged, than were directly impaled.

Most of the fish that Kono did not want were brightly coloured. Those colours suggested poison or unpalatability. At least in that instance, they were of value to their owners as warning coloration.

It was through Carney that I first made close acquaintance with the surgeon fish, who carries a lancet at the base of his tail; the coffer fish, whose skeleton is mostly soft cartilage

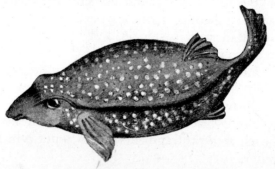

and who is held together by his box-like exterior; and the *vache de mer*, who with his horns and large eyes strangely re-

sembles a cow. Kitchee brought them to me in an old enamelled basin, and many an hour I spent in trying to register their forms on paper. She brought them faster than I could draw them, and though in many cases I made attempts to record the colours in actual pigment, I find that more often than not my note-book has black-and-white sketches followed by notes which give but faint hints of the ever startling colouring. There were chevrons on the head, circular patches near the tail, parallel bars from head to tail, herring-bone patterns across the belly; and they were of every conceivable colour, each combination more surprising than the last, with almost always an accent of seemingly irrelevant emphasis in the make-up.

One day James Norman Hall, part author of those films *Mutiny on the 'Bounty'*, *Hurricane*, etc., who lives permanently on Tahiti, suggested that I should go with him to Tetiaroa, a low coral island some twenty miles to the north. It took us several days to persuade the crew of the schooner to leave the cinema at Papeete, for a new film had just arrived by the mail boat, and the men insisted on seeing it several times over. Eventually, however, we did manage to get away, one evening, and after sailing all night with a fair wind we woke next morning to see a long, low line of palms on the horizon. Two hours later we had dropped over the side of the schooner into a surf boat and were heading for the reef.

The entrances to the lagoons vary at different islands: some are wide and easy of negotiation, as at Tahiti and Moorea; others have a narrow channel, in and out of which the tide surges; while at many of the low atolls there is no boat pass at all, and the only way of reaching land is by surf-riding the reef. This was the case at Tetiaroa. As we pulled towards the island, rising and falling with the swell, we could see at one moment a white trail of foam as the wave broke over the reef ahead, at the next a yawning abyss of water through which we were rushing at a most unpleasant speed towards a bristling wall of coral.

B

As we neared the reef and the rowers hung on their oars, waiting for the right wave to carry us over, we were greeted by shouts from a party of islanders who had waded through the lagoon to meet us. They stood in the breaking water on the edge of the reef ready to lend a hand. It was well for us that they had done so, for the chosen wave lacked force, and during one long agonizing moment we remained, suspended between sky and sea, balanced precariously on the wrong side of a jagged precipice. Fortunately a rope was thrown and held, and thus only were our children rescued from orphanage. The next mountain of water carried us to safety, and we were towed in state to the shore.

Tetiaroa is typical of the seventy or more atolls which lie to the north-east of Tahiti. It consists of a number of islets rising but a few feet above the general level of a ring of coral which encircles a lagoon. Outside this ring is an area of calm water which is again enclosed by a barrier reef of coral on which the surf is for ever breaking, and beyond which the sea sinks precipitously to almost unknown depths. There are therefore two lagoons, a central one whose water is often brackish and an encircling one whose water is clear and sparkling. It was when making our entry into the latter of these that we so nearly met with disaster.

This island, on which little more than coco-nut palms now grows, was at one time part of the ancestral property of the royal house of Tahiti, whose chiefs used it not only as a place of quiet and rest from political disturbances, but also as a resort where the ladies of the court could practise the fashionable art of fattening. Beauty, in the eyes of a Tahitian, consisted in being stout and fair. Those were royal characteristics. Any one who was thin was obviously ill. To-day native belles keep out of the sun as much as possible to preserve the 'fairness' of their skins. It seems odd to them that white visitors should be so anxious to get brown.

Legend hints that King Pomare I used to retire to Tetiaroa to hold his 'heathen orgies' when, owing to the influence of the missionaries, it was no longer politic to continue such observances on the main island. But over and above fattening females and heterodox theology, the island was famed for fish; so important, indeed, was this item of its produce considered, that by royal decree no bread-fruit might be grown on the atoll. In this way the inhabitants were compelled to bring their fish to Tahiti to barter for the fruit. To-day the island is almost uninhabited, but the glory of the reef remains the same.

Tetiaroa, atoll of five islets, what do I remember of it? Palm-trees, of course, and a thick fern-like scrub growing everywhere. No land more than a few feet above sea-level. There was a white tern that flew threateningly at our heads, as terns do the whole world over. There were mosquitoes at night. There were flies in the daytime. Over and above all other memories and impressions there were fish.

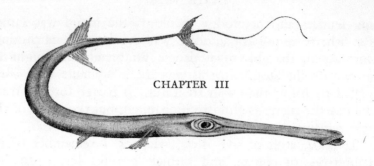

CHAPTER III

LONDON

WHEN, too, I eventually sailed from Tahiti, I had but one big regret—the *reef* I'd left behind me. Throughout the journey home, throughout the days that followed, my mind was ever harking back to those clear waters and all that they contained.

With the idea, then, of building up a few atolls of scientific knowledge in the ocean of my ignorance, I visited again and again the Natural History Museum at South Kensington. Within those walls I met with a perfect hurricane of information, an encyclopaedic storm in which sharks, turtles, sword-fish, angel fish, sponges, corals, squids, and starfish ricocheted off each other and gyrated around me. Many a day and many an hour I stood before the glass-fronted cases. There was the little fish *Pomocanthus imperator* who, in his youth, wears a livery of white concentric circles on black, and then by varied transformations eventually changes it to parallel yellow lines on brown; there was the European eel who must travel to the West Indies to celebrate its nuptials; there were remoras who attach themselves to sharks by sucking-disks, and travel the world in such grim company; there was fierasfer, a small eel-like fish whose notion of life is to insert himself within the hinder end of a sea-slug's gut, and only emerge for food and exercise. There was no end to the diversity of habit or strangeness of taste.

As time went on I got hold of various scientific treatises. Professor Reighard, in his paper from the Tortugas Marine Biological Station, proved not only that fish recognize different colours, but that they have memory. He showed, for example, that when 'an inconspicuous fish which serves normally as the food of the grey snapper is given an artificial warning colour and at the same time rendered unpalatable it is, after a brief experience, no longer taken as food.' His experiments need not concern us here more than to say that the normally inconspicuous fish were dyed vermilion, yellow, green, sky-blue, and purple, and filled with such unsavoury condiments as red pepper, strong ammonia, or carbon disulphide. It was observed that within a very short time each colour be-came associated in the fish's mind with certain unpleasant characteristics just as our minds have, through remote ex-perience, become apprehensive of a certain blueness on beefsteak, or redness in a wayside berry.

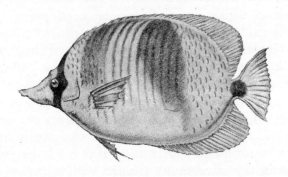

Dr. C. H. Townsend, in *Zoologica*, vol. ix, no. 9, published by the New York Zoological Society, describes the various changes in colour which have been observed in the fish under his care. Speaking of the Nassau grouper, he says: 'Eight phases of coloration are sometimes observed. In one the fish is uniformly dark; in another creamy white. In a third it is dark above, with white underparts. In a fourth the upper part of the body is sharply banded, the lower pure white. A fifth phase shows dark bands, the whole fish taking on a light-brown coloration, while in a sixth the fish is pale, with all dark markings tending to disappear. The seventh phase shows a light-coloured fish with the body sharply banded and mottled with black, while in the eighth the body is dusky above, white below, with a median black band from head to tail.'

The same writer describing the blue tang says: 'Two striking phases of coloration are assumed, one a dark blue, the other a creamy white. The blue phase is the one usually seen, since it is assumed whenever the fish is in the least disturbed by visitors passing the tank, and this lasts all day long. The other phase is seldom seen until evening, when the fish may settle down toward the white sand bottom and take on a ghostly whiteness, the blue colour remaining only as a narrow border on the fins. Any disturbance instantly brings back the blue colour.' These are but two examples from about thirty species which he has described.

But besides the fish, I became intensely aware of that variety of sea anemone which can secrete for itself an external skeleton of lime, and which is known as the coral polyp. It was given this name by French naturalists who when they first saw the tentacles of growing coral associated them with the octopus known to them as *le poulpe*, from the Latin *polypus*, meaning many-footed. In some cases no bigger than a pin's head, in others having a diameter as large as a three-penny bit, while in a few cases approximating to the size of a saucer and the appearance of an inverted mushroom, this organism, so simple in construction that it consists of hardly more than a digestive cavity fringed with tentacles, has yet built up innumerable islands in all the tropic seas, and vast areas of protecting reef along the shores of continents.

Every subject that I studied brought another into view. The common blue mussel opened up vistas of pearl-oysters and giant clams. The trumpet shell of our own shores led the way to the great conch, whose deep sound I had heard so often at night when the Tahitian fishermen signalled to each other on the reef. Even the worms who chew the dead coral and pass it from their bodies in fine particles commanded interest, for what would tropic isles be without their sand?

Weeks passed by, months, and even years, until one day in the summer of 1937 I leaned over a ship's rail and watched the suburbs of Liverpool and the pier at New Brighton fade into a mist on the horizon, as we headed for the west and Bermuda.

Gulls, hundreds of them, watching for scraps, floated through the air around us, now with one eye turned downwards, now with the other. They perched on the boats and on the rigging, leaning forward on their wide feet to keep their balance against the wind. Distrustful of passengers, they showed no fear of the sailors.

'I suppose you 're glad to be at sea again,' I said to a sailor.

'There 's only one thing makes me glad,' he said, 'and that 's to be walking up Bold Street along o' the missus, looking in the shop windows, and going to the pictures after. It 'll be three months now afore we does it again.'

Before sailing I had presented myself at the South Kensington Museum to offer my services, should there be any small specimen that I might collect for them on my travels. One of the staff was immediately interested and led me by devious passages and flights of steps to his private room. There, with great solemnity, he communicated to me the fact that his collection was almost complete, that indeed, it only wanted three specimens, and that they were all to be found in the western Atlantic. Then he added that what he needed were three whales. Seeing a slight look of bewilderment on my features, he went on to say that he would be happy to compromise if I could bring him even the heads and skeletons. When I explained that I was travelling light he reduced his demands still further to dolphins.

Now the dolphin has great misfortune in his nomenclature. The creature commonly called by that name, and famed among sailors for its dying colours, is not a dolphin at all. It is a scaly fish of the family Coryphaenidae. The true dolphin bearing the escutcheon of the Delphinidae is a mammal, who, like the whales, the seals, and the dugongs, has taken to an aquatic life because it suited him best. He has lungs like the rest of us, and the bones of his flippers are very much more akin to our hands than they are to the fins of a fish. Of his tribe are the porpoises who pursue their leisurely and sportive way about our shores. Fortunately for me, it

appeared that the specimens required had their habitat considerably south of Bermuda, so that the chances of my needing another suit-case became considerably reduced.

No man starts alone on a long sea journey without optimism as to who may share his table. On earlier voyages I had been for the most part lucky, but this time it seemed that I was to be haunted by that joke in the museum, for sitting opposite to me was a leviathan of a man who ran out a line of fifty-eight inches round his waist and turned the scale at twenty-four stone. For the first time in many years I felt physically small, and humbled, with my miserable eighteen stone dwindled to an appearance of chronic malnutrition. Before that man came aboard carpenters had made special adjustments to his bunk; when he put foot on the gangway all other passengers were held back till he was safely on deck.

At La Pallice, the port of La Rochelle, where we called for a few hours one morning, he suggested that we should share a taxi to the town. We did so. My share was small. Back again on the ship I lay in a deck-chair and had all an infant's delight in recognizing my own limbs. Slowly, so slowly, they recovered consciousness. And as I sat there I soliloquized to myself about the ship. Where had the oak of the rails and the pine of the decks come from? How many years had they taken to grow? In what dense forest? I thought of the rain that had fallen on them and dripped from their leaves; the insects, blindly purposeful, who had lived in their bark; the ill-mannered birds careless of what lived below.

And the metal of the rails, of the plates. Whence was it dug? Whose were the hands that wielded the drills? What men tended the furnaces? Had they wives, children, complexes? While they tended the monstrous hammers beating out these plates, were their hearts quickening at the thought of some clandestine meeting, or had they the pains of jealousy shooting through their bellies?

And the sea, 'so charming' on its surface. How romantic the spray in one's face, the ozone in the air, the flying fish breaking from the waves at the bow. But, at sixty feet down, how different? And at six hundred? And at six thousand, giant squids fighting with sperm whales in the dark shades. . . .

Did you know why salmon fishers need a boiled shrimp as a lure in fresh water? Because when salmon go to the sea they feed at great depths, and at great depths the shrimps are red, not green as we see them by our shores.

Down in those waters there is inky darkness and the temperature everywhere is only barely above freezing-point. There is no vegetation. The sea floor is covered with thick soft ooze. Yet, even at twelve thousand feet, life is abundant, and there is the same struggle for existence as elsewhere. In those waters there are fish that have developed luminous organs that can be flashed on and off at will. There are others that have developed 'telescopic' eyes, that they may catch the faintest glimmer of those lights. There are fish whose stomachs are capable of such expansion that they can swallow other fish larger than their own normal size. Strangest of all, perhaps, there is a species in which the mature male, after a free-swimming youth, becomes not only attached to the female but completely fused to it. Its head grows into one part or another of its mate, the head, the abdomen, or the side. Then the jaws and gills become atrophied, and from that on the whole system of the male is an integral part, a mere appendage, of the female. Such conditions are an ideal of matrimony to *some* people.

'Weather's a bit dry,' said the purser, appearing behind me.

'Come and join us,' called Miss Angel, as we set a course for the bar. 'Mickey is telling us a wonderful story.'

Mickey was always telling wonderful stories. He had a broken nose and a drooping eyelid, which gave the effect of a perpetual wink, and he was as lean and tough as a wire hawser. He had served his time in sail, been engineer on a tramp, then took to mining, and how he had the idea that once he got to Callao his fortune would be made.

'What's the yarn?' I asked as we sat down.

'Just told it,' said Mickey.

'Tell it again.'

'Only happened once.'

'I think it was perfectly awful,' said Miss Angel.

'What was?' we asked.

'He fell overboard and the captain wouldn't pick him up.'

'He did pick me up,' interposed Mickey.

'He was rude to you,' purred Miss Angel.

'He called me up on the poop and he said, "You been overboard?" I said, "Yes, sir." Then he said, "Who the hell gave you permission to leave the ship? You go aloft again," he said, "and dry your clothes and wait there till I give you orders to come down, and don't try any more diving tricks."'

'An absolute beast,' said the Angel.

'A damn fine man,' said Mickey. 'When we arrived in port he gave me half a crown out of his own pocket and said, "You go ashore and have a ruddy good swim at the baths."'

Miss Angel purred, and sipped her 'sidecar.' She was buxom, blonde, and generally wore blue, so we called her Blue Angel. On the first evening out, as we leaned over the rail together, she told me how interested she was in art, in wood-cuts particularly, had indeed done some herself— or was it lino cuts? She wasn't quite sure.

She had stood closer and let her arm touch mine: our feet met on the rail. She did *so* admire artists. Did I understand? She did so admire tall men, and men with beards. Did I only draw fish? Did I ever draw people? She would so like to be drawn. Did I understand?

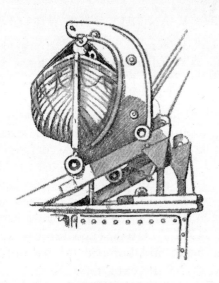

CHAPTER IV

BERMUDA

THE ship ploughed on, and the weather grew warmer. Blue Angel purred to each officer and passenger in turn. She did so admire sailors, engineers, doctors, business men. It must be wonderful to live on the sea, in the great wide spaces, in a hospital, in a city. Did they understand? The heart-line on her palm must have been like chain-stitch.

One day a family of false killer whales, with a young calf close to its mother, showed their velvety backs for a few moments on our beam, and I thought of D. H. Lawrence's lines:

'There they blow, there they blow, hot wild white breath
    out of the sea!
And they rock, and they rock, through the sensual ageless
    ages
On the depths of the seven seas. . . .'

These false killers are easily distinguishable from the true killer by their smaller size and the lack of any white on their body. The killer's back is black, its belly white. The false killer rarely exceeds eighteen feet, whereas the killer may be up to thirty feet in length. Their feeding habits, too, are different. The false killer lives, for the most part, on cuttle-fish, but the killer is out for mammals and the larger birds, such as penguins. Again and again stories come to us of the terrible wolf-like hunting of these killers, stories that tell of packs of them hounding down dolphins, seals, walrus, sea-lions, even the larger baleen whales that may run to three times their own size. On the north-west coast of Alaska it is be-lieved that the same spirit can be a wolf on land and a killer whale in the water. And they are credited with immense cunning. When Mr. Ponting was at work with his camera on the Terra Nova Antarctic expedition it was killers that came up underneath and bumped the ice until it broke, in their efforts to get at the explorers.

Mr. Cherry-Garrard in *The Worst Journey in the World* gives the following description of the incident: 'Some six or seven killer whales, old and young, were skirting the fast floe edge ahead of the ship; they seemed excited and dived rapidly, almost touching the floe. As we watched, they suddenly appeared astern, raising their snouts out of water. I had heard weird stories of these beasts, but had never associated serious danger with them. Close to the water's edge lay the wire stern rope of the ship, and our two Esquimaux dogs were tethered to this. I did not think of connecting the movement of the whales with this fact, and seeing them so close I shouted to Ponting, who was standing abreast of the ship. He seized his camera and ran towards the floe edge to get a close picture of the beasts, which had momentarily disappeared. The next moment the whole floe under him and the dogs heaved up and split into fragments. One could hear the booming noise as the whales rose under the ice and struck it with their backs. Whale after whale rose under the ice, setting it rocking fiercely; luckily Ponting kept his feet and was able to fly to security. By an extraordinary chance also, the splits had been made around and between the dogs, so that neither of them fell into the water. Then it was clear that the whales shared our astonishment, for one after an-other their huge hideous heads shot vertically into the air through the cracks which they had made. As they reared them to a height of six or eight feet it was possible to see their tawny head markings, their small glistening eyes, and their terrible array of teeth—by far the largest and most terrifying in the world. There cannot be a doubt that they looked up to see what had happened to Ponting and the dogs. The latter were horribly frightened and strained to their chains, whining; the head of one killer must certainly have been within five feet of one of the dogs. . . . Of course we have known well that killer whales continually skirt the edge of the floes and that they would undoubtedly snap up any one who was unfortunate enough to fall into the water; but the facts that they could display such deliberate cunning, that they were able to break ice of such thickness (at least 2 feet), and that they could act in unison, were a revelation to us.'

Again, Dr. F. D. Ommanney in *South Latitude*, when describing the return from a whale hunt, writes of these killers: 'They were making after us, making after the carcases we towed. As they gained upon us with rushing, swooping dives through the water, we could see their black shapes beneath the surface. They made one or two swift sweeps towards the mouths of the dead whales from which the tongues lolled out. There was something terrible and sinister in the rush they made, the tigers of the sea.'

The larger species of whales, such as the blue whale and the sperm whale, either of which may reach a hundred feet in length, are not only the greatest of living creatures in size, they are also greater than any creature known ever to have existed. Small wonder then that many exaggerations and fanciful stories of their size have come down to us from the past. Pliny tells us that the whale is so long and broad as to take up four acres of land. Another account gives nine hundred feet as the length. One of the most charming legends, from an ancient bestiary, tells us that:

'When the whale hungreth sore, he casteth out of his mouth a vapour, that smelleth as the smell of amber; and fish have liking in that smell, and for the odour and smell of that vapour, they go into the whale's mouth, and be so deceived and eaten. Also in this fish earthy matter hath more mastery than watery, and therefore he is soon great and fat; and so in age for greatness of body, on his ridge powder and earth is gathered, and so digged together that herbs and bushes and small trees grow thereon; so that the great fish seemeth an island. And if shipmen come unwarily thereby, unneath they scape without peril, for he throweth up so much water out of his mouth upon the ship, that he overturneth it sometime or drowneth it. And also he is so huge in quantity that when he is taken, all the country is the better for the taking. Also he loveth his whelps with a wonder love, and leadeth them about in the sea long time. And if it happeth that his whelps be let with heaps of gravel and by default of water he taketh much water in his mouth, and throweth upon them, and delivereth them in that wise from peril. And he setteth them alway between himself and the sun on the more sicher side. And when strong tempest ariseth, while his whelps be tender and young, he swalloweth them up into his own womb; and when the tempest is gone, and fair weather come, then he casteth them up whole and sound. Also against the whale fighteth a fish of serpent's kind, and is venomous, as a crocodile; and then other fish come to the whale's tail, and if the whale be overcome, the other fish die. And if the venomous fish may not overcome the whale, then he throweth out of his jaws into the water a fumous smell most stinking, and the whale throweth out of his mouth a sweet smelling smoke, and putteth off the stinking smell, and defendeth and saveth himself in that manner wise.'

Legends similar to this occur in many other medieval texts, notably in *Physiologus*, the metrical bestiary of Bishop Theobald who from A.D. 1022 to 1035 was abbot of Monte Cassino, that monastery which has but recently suffered such grievous damage. The idea of the whale being mistaken for an island occurs again and again in early literature. We find it in the *True History* of Lucian, in the *Voyage* of St. Brandan, and in the adventures of Sinbad the Sailor. In a twelfth-century manuscript in the British Museum there is an illustration showing a ship beside a large fish, on whose back there is a fire with a black pot resting on it: one of the mariners, balancing himself on the fish's head, blows the fire with a bellows.   A similar picture is to be found in an early manuscript in the Bodleian Library.

Flying fish broke in all directions from our bows.   Always unexpected, from here, from there, scintillating with light they skim the surface, gliding, wheeling, bouncing off a wave crest, gliding again, then dropping back into the water with a splash.

So the ship moved steadily westward day and night, the sun rose and set on a calm sea, and the passengers' lives were circumscribed by a perimeter of meals and deck quoits.

One evening I got talking to a young stoker who had come on to the after-deck for a breath of air.   He was wearing a pair of much-stained dungaree trousers and a torn singlet, and the perspiration from his face was running into the greasy 'sweat-rag' tied around his neck.   He told me that he had recently spent six months in London on an engineering course.

'How did you get on?' I asked.

'Quids in,' he said; 'twenty-two Prom. concerts.   Lose yourself for two bob a time.'

On the fourteenth day we reached Bermuda, and almost before the anchor had stirred the sea floor I was appropriated by the uncrowned monarch of the island.   We reached the Yacht Club at 9.30 a.m.   By 9.33 I had been made a member of the club.   At 10.15 I was poured on to the train for St. George's.

On arrival at the biological station, where I was to work, a more serious vein of thought was awakened in me, and little by little I settled down to the main business of my travelling.

As I have already said, it was my ambition to get on closer terms with the fish, and to meet them, so to speak, on their own level, and one of my chief reasons for coming to Bermuda was to make use of the diving apparatus belonging to the marine research station; I was anxious, too, to make drawings under the water.   When first considering this possibility I had thought of taking down copper plates prepared for etching, but when I mentioned the subject to Cyril Pearce, a colleague of mine at Reading University, where I was then working, he suggested that I should try drawing on xylonite, a waterproof substance not unlike celluloid.   Sheets of this, when roughened with sandpaper, take a pencil as pleasantly as paper.   I had therefore brought a supply with me, as well as some of those thick sticks of graphite that are usually supplied as refills for sketching pencils.   Instead of their normal wooden casing, which would have come to pieces in the water, I fitted them into rubber tubing.   By that means I hoped that my hands would remain clean, and smudges on the drawings be avoided.

The diving apparatus consists of a helmet, a length of hose-pipe, and an air pump.   The helmet, with weights hung on to overcome the buoyancy of the air within, rests on the diver's shoulders, and is not attached to his body in any way. Under the water its weight becomes imperceptible, and at any moment it can be lifted and thrown clear of the wearer. Then with a kick to the sea-floor the diver rises quickly to the surface.   The pressure of the air within the helmet is kept up by the pump, operated from the launch overhead. Provided the man at the job does not go to sleep in the sun, there is sufficient pressure to prevent the water rising above chin level.   The head, therefore, is the only part of the body that is enclosed in air, the surplus air escaping at shoulder level.   The rest of the body is in free contact with the water.

My first dive was an experimental one from the pier. 'Stand on the ladder,' said Edwin Whitfield, who was in charge of operations, 'and I'll put the helmet over your head.   Then I'll add the weights; then I'll start pumping. Go down the ladder, then,' he said, 'until you meet the bottom, turn round and make your way to the end of the pier, and on the far side you will find a deep hole.   Drop into that and see how you get on.'

As I stepped down that ladder, with the noise of the pump

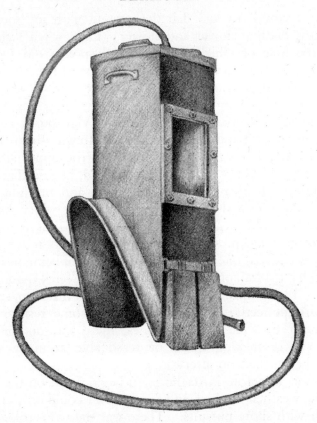

echoing down the hose-pipe, and the waves splashing against the window of the helmet so that I could see neither land nor water, I wondered why I had ever left home. But once below the surface my feelings changed. My ears ceased throbbing, I breathed easily, I forgot the noise of the pump, and I could see clearly.

From the hard iron rung of the ladder I stepped on to the soft ooze of the sea-floor. It was like being in some great cathedral lit by pale green glass. I moved silently, as through a vast nave whose aisles were lost in mists—to paraphrase Edwin Arnold, 'veil after veil lifting and other veils beyond.' Brightly coloured fish, momentarily glinting, were like the tinted panes of heraldry that sometimes decorate a light.

But as I reached deeper water my feet seemed to lose their

hold. I could pat and dab the ground with my toes, but progress became slower and slower. Only when I skidded into the hole of which Whitfield had spoken did I gather any speed. It was even more difficult when I tried to return. Then I could get no grip at all with my feet. I felt like a restive horse, pawing the ground, but reined in so that I could not move. Eventually, by striking out vigorously with my arms, as in swimming, and using my drawing-board as an auxiliary fin, I did manage to return to the upper air.

On explaining my difficulty to Whitfield, he said that I was too light. He then went to the stores and brought forth some twenty pounds' weight of lead piping, which he suggested I should wear as a waist-belt. So, thus accoutred, I descended again. This time I was able to move about below as easily as one walks on land, in spite of being weighted down by a total of some hundred and twenty pounds of metal. I tried drawing on the xylonite, and that, too, seemed to work perfectly. Though there was some resistance of the water to wide sweeping lines, there was no difficulty whatever in making notes of reasonable accuracy which could be worked on afterwards.

All was therefore in readiness to begin work on the reefs. But the weather was bad, and for a week I could only employ myself with shore pursuits. There was the red cardinal bird to be seen searching for insects in the bark of the cedar-trees. There was the minute ground-dove gathering seeds on the dry soil. There was the bluebird of Bermuda, reflecting every tint of sea and sky as it flitted through the sub-tropical vegetation.

A Negro, to whom I spoke, hoped that I was enjoying my holiday.

'I'm not on holiday,' I said, 'I'm working.'

'Why, sah,' he said, 'I thought by yo' looks you was gen'leman o' leesure.'

'Far from it,' I said.

'Waal, that good fo' you, now sah. Too much leesure bad fo' any man, gen'leman or no gen'leman.'

Even so I had my moments of relaxation, and during one

of them I collected the recipe for 'planters' punch.' Here it is:

> One of sour (one part *fresh* lime juice).
> Two of sweet (two parts sugar).
> Three of strong (three parts old Jamaica rum).
> Four of weak (four parts water and ice).
> Add a dash of bitters. Shake well. Serve very
> cold in a tall glass with cracked ice. Add
> a cherry.

Apropos of which, I studied one learned professor while he studied crustacea. To assist him in his work he consumed large quantities of rum, but, lest that gracious aid to knowledge should prove too exuberant in its action, this man of science kept his supply of liquor in such a place that he could only reach it when standing in his bath. The bath was kept permanently full of cold water, and the professor maintained that by these constant restorative immersions of his feet he could maintain that perfect mental equilibrium necessary to the higher forms of research.

I spoke, too, with an aged harpooner who had 'squared his yards, coiled down his ropes, and was waiting for the last signal to let go his anchor.' He was standing outside his cottage with one foot on a monstrous bone and he tried to tell me stories of the past. But he spoke in a dialect which for the most part I could not understand and, for all that I could do, his legends must die with him.

Whales were at one time plentiful in Bermudan waters, but through excessive hunting and slaughter they are now rare. Silvester Jourdain, in *A Discovery of the Barmudas, otherwise called the Ile of Divils*, 1610, tells us: 'There are also great plenty of whales, which I conceave are very easie to be killed, for they come so usually, and ordinarily to the shore, that we heard them oftentimes in the night a bed; and have seene many of them neare the shore, in the day time.' With Jourdain on that same expedition was another, one William Strachey, who afterwards, like Jourdain, published his experiences. Of the islands, on which he was wrecked, he writes: 'The dangerous and dreaded Iland, or rather Ilands of the Bermuda . . . so terrible to all that ever touched on them, and such tempests, thunders, and other fearefull objects are seene and heard about them, that they be called commonly The Devil's Ilands, and are feared and avoyded of all sea travellers alive, above any other place in the world . . . it being counted of most that they can be no habitation for Men, but rather given over to Devils and wicked spirits.'

Scholars, the world over, are agreed that it was from the writings of these two men that Shakespeare drew much of his local colour for *The Tempest*. One example should suffice us here. Strachey, describing the 'most dreadfull Tempest' which overwhelmed them with 'an hell of darknesse' and crashes of thunder that 'overmastered the sences of all,' writes of 'an apparition of a little round light, like a faint Starre, trembling and streaming along with a sparkeling blaze, halfe the height upon the Maine Mast, and shooting sometimes from Shroud to Shroud, tempting to settle as it were upon any of the foure Shrouds: and for three or foure houres together, or rather more, halfe the night it kept with us; running sometimes along the Maine-yard to the very end, and then returning.' Shakespeare makes Ariel say:

> 'I boarded the king's ship; now on the beak,
> Now in the waist, the deck, in every cabin,
> I flamed amazement: sometime I 'ld divide,
> And burn in many places; on the topmast,
> The yards and bowsprit, would I flame distinctly,
> Then meet and join. Jove's lightnings, the precursors
> O' the dreadful thunder-claps, more momentary
> And sight-outrunning were not . . .'

Richard Stafford, writing from Bermuda about the year 1668, describes the spiders' webs that he saw on the island. He says: 'Here are Spiders, that spin their Webs betwixt Trees standing 7 or 8 Fathom asunder; and they do their Work by spirting their Web into the Air, where the Wind carries it from Tree to Tree. This Web, when finished, will snare a Bird as big as a Thrush.' He referred to the great

silk-spider, some five to six inches across the outstretched
legs, and of a reddish or chestnut brown with silver and gold
spots on back and abdomen.   His description is not exaggerated.   We find parallels in many other countries.   From
North Borneo comes the account of a bird as large as a gold-
finch 'fast entangled in the web of a spider of the genus
Nephilia' (the same genus).   In Moseley's notes on the *Challenger* expedition we read of a 'strong and healthy glossy-
starling caught fast in a yellow-spider's web.'   That was in
the East Indies.   From the West Indies, Madagascar, and
Ceylon there come similar statements.   Bates, in his *Naturalist
on the River Amazons*, tells of a large hairy spider of the genus
Mygale.   He says: 'I was attracted by a movement of the
monster on a tree-trunk; it was close beneath a deep crevice
in the tree, across which was stretched a dense white web.
The lower part of the web was broken, and two small birds,
finches, were entangled in the pieces; they were about the
size of the English siskin, and I judged the two to be male
and female.   One of them was quite dead, the other lay under
the belly of the spider not quite dead. . . .'   Paul Fountain,
in *The River Amazon* (1914), gives a more recent account,
telling of a spider that spins its web, not vertically but hori-
zontally, so that birds darting upwards are caught.   Small
birds such as the gem-bird, the ant-bird, and humming birds
are entangled, and the spider treats them as the common
spider of our homes treats a fly, sucking every drop of blood
and moisture from the bodies and then dropping the almost
shapeless remains clear of the web, where they are soon
demolished by ants and beetles.

But an even more surprising fact about such webs is that
they can be, and are, used as fishing nets.   H. B. Guppy, in
The Solomon Islands and their Natives (1887), tells how, being
anxious to get some small fish from a brook, his native atten-
dants bent a twig into a loop and spread over it a strong
spider-web from the nearby weeds.   Floating this on the water
they sprinkled it with ants' eggs and grubs.   The small fish,
apparently not seeing the transparent web, jumped at the bait
and soon had their heads entangled in the meshes.   William

Deane, in *Fijian Society* (1921), writes: 'A piece of reed was taken and bent into a circle, the ends being firmly tied. Afterwards a short handle was attached. The operator went into the woods and found strong spider-webs in which he waved the bent reed many times until it became quite covered with them. The handle was taken away and the reed-hoop, so enveloped, was laid on the top of the water in a stream, where it floated. The fishermen then put into it small grasshoppers and flies. . . . The fish rose like trout, and in their eagerness to get the bait were caught by the gills and fins in the spider-web.' Other accounts come from the Trobriand Islands, from the New Hebrides, and from New Guinea where, it is stated, fish up to a pound in weight can be caught by this method.

Though the sea was too rough for diving, it was not too rough for us to put down fish traps. These were made of wire netting, stretched over a frame of bamboos. Sometimes we would get a dozen or more individuals, among whom there might be three or four different species. At other times it might only be a single big rock-fish, whose well-filled paunch suggested only too clearly why it was alone. On one occasion we had positive proof of our suspicions, for either from nerves or the movement of the launch, a two-foot groper was unable to retain its appropriation, and, halfway home, we discovered a smaller fish in the tank beside him.

On the first calm day we headed the launch for the reef in Castle Harbour. The sky was a vibrant blue. The sea was smooth as the proverbial mirror. Shoals of fry, leaping to avoid pursuers, sprang from the water like jets of fine spray, rising and falling in a series of glittering arches. Having reached our intended position and chosen a suitable site, we put out anchors fore and aft, for an essential condition of the operation is that the boat from which one works should be stationary. It might have very unpleasant results for the diver, if, with the swinging of the vessel, he got dragged against the coral. After the anchors were in position, a ladder was lowered over the side with a weighted rope dropping from its end. Soon I was down below.

Here the water was as clear as English daylight. I had dropped into the centre of a ring of coral which grew from a considerable depth, though where I stood there was but fifteen to twenty feet of water above me. I walked on clean

sand. Pillars and pylons of coral encircled me. I was in a natural amphitheatre, an arena where each day and all day carnival is held. Generally speaking, the fish showed little fear of me when I was under water. A few glanced at the strange invader from a safe distance and then moved to a safer one, but the majority, hundreds of them, crowded around me. There were blue angels and yellow grunts, sergeant-majors, trigger fish and porgies, four-eyes and demoiselles. The angels came and looked through the window of the helmet, the pudding wives and blue-heads swam between my legs, and the sergeant-majors nibbled at my shoulders. I often had to wave my arms to drive away these insistent inquirers. In and out through the crevices of the coral, and under the overhanging brainstones they came and went, moving without apparent effort, while the blue and gold clumps of iridescent weed swayed in the swell.

The blue angels, deep laterally compressed fish with long filaments to their tail and fins, have become the mascot of Bermuda. Varying in colour from cerulean blue to deep cobalt, they grow to a length of eighteen inches. They are as ubiquitous on the reefs as their models are in the shops. The yellow grunts, up to about a foot in length, take their name, like twelve other Bermudian species, from the grunting noise which they produce when captured. The sergeant-majors, smaller fish and not conspicuous in colour, are so designated from the numerous vertical stripes across their bodies. There are fourteen different species of trigger fish to be found in these waters, varying from the modest little two-inch file fish to the truly regal queen trigger. All have the distinguishing characteristic of a long sharp spine as the first item of their dorsal fin. The queen is as haughty and magnificent a creature as one could find in any waters, with her exotic blue markings on the head and the spreading purple flounces of her fins and tail. The pudding wives, for whose name I can give no reason, and the blue-heads, whose title needs no explaining, are both more or less 'normally' shaped fish, the blue-head being rather more elongate than the other. They have this quality in common that scarcely ever will one see two specimens, of either species, that are alike in colour. A pudding wife may be a combination of lemon gold, brown, and white, spotted and striped with emerald green and blue, almost metallic in lustre; or it may be mainly blue or mainly bronze with stripes of white, yellow, or orange. In the blue-head, varieties of coloration baffle description, males differ from females, mature fish from those less mature; colours assumed during the day are different from those exhibited at night. And between any two distinctive phases there are innumerable transitionary ones.

My second drawing was made in somewhat similar surroundings. Again great spheres and hemispheres of coral raised themselves one on the other, sea fans and gorgonias

(flexible branching corals) waved in the current, and fish abounded. Each time that I went down I made a drawing. There was no need to wander about and search for a subject; wherever I looked there was something new to draw. The strange thing was that when I came back to the surface I found that during my time below I had forgotten all rules of perspective and other dicta of the art schools, and that I had drawn everything in the proportion of its importance to me. In the upper world of air we have accustomed ourselves to make subconscious adjustments in our vision, so that an elephant seen a mile away still conjures up an idea of something large, though its actual dimensions on our retina may be no bigger than those of the fly on our boot. Under the water all these adjustments vanished, and if a particularly interesting small fish passed in the distance, I found that in my drawing it was depicted as very much larger than some dull fellow twice the size who happened to be near at hand. This suggests a parallel with primitive art, where objects were drawn on cave wall or canvas according to their importance to the artist, and not according to mathematics and laws of optics.

In many places outside the harbour the gorgonias predominate, covering the sea-floor with their growth. Dropping down among them I could see, in all directions, romantic alley-ways opening to the ocean beyond. The water here was even clearer than in the harbour, and all life sparkled with iridescence.

CHAPTER V

CORAL ISLANDS

BEFORE we go any farther we must consider in rather more detail what this amazing organism called a polyp may be, and how it is that through its agency not only have some of the most romantic places in the world been built, but some of the greatest shipping disasters have occurred. All over the warmer waters of the Pacific Ocean, from the East Indies and Great Barrier Reef of Australia to the Paumotu Archipelago, all through the West Indies, in the Indian Ocean, and in the Red Sea we find this ubiquitous organism building up isles of enchantment, or reefs whereon proud ships are wrecked. Only on the western shores of the great continents is it absent, for there flow cold currents from the poles.

Cross-section of a polyp of coral known as *Lobophyllia*, reproduced direct from the coral itself.

The polyp itself is, as we have said, a form of sea anemone, similar in many ways to those of our own shores, but having the power to abstract lime from sea-water and deposit it as a calcareous skeleton about its base and sides, as well as forming radiating septa which act as protection for the soft tissues within. It differs, however, from the anemone in that it reproduces by budding, very much as a tree shoots forth its branches, and it is in this way that whole colonies are formed, which are the chief elements in reef construction. As the oak, the ash, or the chestnut throws out its branches, each after its own kind, so also the various corals send out their buds in a manner characteristic of their species; but just as the oak-trees on windswept coasts differ from those in sheltered parks, so, also, each coral is automatically pruned by the conditions in which it finds itself. In deep water, long stems may reach towards the surface, as straight and bare of branches as the pollarded poplars of France, while in rough water, where the surf breaks on the reef, the very same variety may be as compact in form as the clipped shrubs that decorate our public gardens.   Only in the sheltered

shallow waters do we get the richest foliation and the full glory of unimpeded growth.

Though intensely prolific in favourable circumstances, the polyp is nevertheless highly sensitive to certain changes of conditions.   A heavy tropical rain storm may, by diluting the surface of the sea, kill all the growing tips of the coral that come within its reach. Similarly, an unusually low tide which leaves the reef exposed for a few hours, as happened a few years ago in the Red Sea, or a sudden reduction of sea temperature such as happened in Bermuda in 1901, may destroy the life over a wide area. Silt is one of the coral's greatest enemies, and the form and structure of the growth of the same species of coral varies considerably in overcoming this menace. It is easy to imagine that where a flat, saucer-like colony finds itself in a muddy area, the edges of it, which are closest to the mud, will be retarded in their development owing to the cilia of the polyps being compelled to spend overtime in removing the debris rather than in obtaining nourishment for their owner. In this way the more centrally situated polyps get a lead, and the general shape of the colony becomes convex, thereby automatically rendering itself less and less vulnerable to the onslaught of the enemy.

It is owing to the fact that reef-building corals cannot flourish below a depth of about thirty fathoms that so much controversy has arisen concerning the formation of reefs and atolls. Darwin proposed the simple explanation that each atoll is now, as it were, the tombstone of a former island.

His theory was that in a past age these islands were high above the sea-level, and that they were surrounded by a fringing reef, which grew up from a comparatively shallow depth. But throughout long epochs of time, and because of movements in the ocean floor, the islands were gradually subsiding, though at such a slow rate that the coral could all the time keep growing at sea-level. Where the water was constantly changing, as on the outer edges of the reef, there the coral grew most strongly; and in course of time an ever-deepening lagoon was formed inside the reef and around the remaining peaks of the island. Finally those peaks sank slowly to oblivion, and the waters of the lagoon flowed over and covered all traces.

This theory was generally accepted until Sir John Murray, after his voyage in H.M.S. *Challenger*, 1872–6, put forward the converse opinion that the coral grew not on a sinking island, but on submarine peaks or mounds which had for the most part been elevated by volcanic agency.

Professor Stanley Gardiner of Cambridge suggests that other corals existing in deep waters, though not reef-builders themselves, may have brought about accumulations of detritus which would in time be near enough to the surface for the reef builders to gain a footing.

Professor A. R. Daly of America has calculated that during the great Ice Age the general level of the equatorial seas was about thirty fathoms lower than it is to-day, and that it may have been at that time that the foundations of many atolls were laid.

It is probable that each of these theories, and others, may

hold true for different islands; for as Dr. C. M. Yonge, who led the Great Barrier Reef expedition of 1928–9, says: 'It is certain that coral reefs have not all been formed in the same way.'

Perhaps it is more interesting for the layman to realize

that reefs and islands are actually being formed to-day just as they were yesterday. Though it may take seven thousand years for some of the slower-growing corals to build a reef a hundred and fifty feet in depth, or perhaps a quarter of that time for some of the quicker-growing species to achieve the same result, nevertheless the activity goes on unceasingly.

And it is not only the exuberant growth of the living polyp which, ramifying everywhere, builds up these great structures. It is the dead coral also. Broken by the waves and reduced to powder by boring molluscs and worms, this serves as cement to bind the whole together; and, burying themselves in it, there are shell-fish who in turn contribute their shells to the general structure. Over it all is deposited a gentle rain of sediment from the sea-water. One day, when the living rock has reached the surface, a floating coco-nut will be arrested in its travels and, taking root, will throw up its leaves. Then begins another cycle. The leaves of the tree will fall and rot, forming humus, and in this humus other seeds, borne by sea and wind, will take root. They in their turn will die and form further soil, and so a new world will come into being on which all the romance and tragedy of human life will find a setting.

CHAPTER VI

THE 'SEABIRD'

ONE day in the launch with Whitfield I asked what had brought him to Bermuda.

'Fish,' he replied, 'same as yourself.'

'What do you want with fish?' I said. 'I thought you were a naval officer.'

'Second officer in the B.I. once, but I wanted to be free; so did Dunch, shipmate of mine, so we cashed in and bought a yacht.'

'And sailed to Bermuda?' I asked.

'Half-way, and got wrecked.'

'Go on. Tell me.'

'Nothing to tell. 'Twas Dunch's idea. Caught me in Antwerp, just back from four years' sweating in the East. He said: "Let's buy a fishing-boat, sail her to Bermuda, catch fish, and make money."

'The idea seemed a good one to me, so we hunted for a boat. But I'd been to every fishing village on the east coast before I found what we wanted in Cowes. The *Seabird*, forty-one years old, and sound, yawl-rigged, forty-eight feet over all, twelve feet beam. We lived in her fo'c'sle and worked like hell from dawn till dark, insulating her main cabin and installing refrigerating machinery in the owner's cabin. For the voyage to Madeira she was rigged with a heavy free-footed trysail with a twelve-foot gaff, and a jib-headed mizzen of the same brick-red canvas.

'God, it was a cold grey day when we headed down Southampton Water, wind north-east. We were logging six and a half knots. Wind freshened next morning, and everything was perfect. Making water a bit fast, we thought; but no matter. What we didn't know was that she 'd been a year in the mud, and that under the copper there wasn't much else but that same mud in her seams. Then we had a south-east gale. It blew all night. We took turns at the pump and tiller, but in spite of continuous pumping the water in her bilge seemed to get no lower. Next morning the water was over the floorboards and the pump choked. The only thing to do was run for Falmouth. What a glorious sail that was! She tore north before the gale with three reefs in the mainsail, the great waves racing up astern. From the trough we could look back and up at great mountains of water; then that wild exhilarating swoop, and we were away up in the breaking crest itself. We reached Falmouth next morning, and when we got the copper off you could see daylight through the seams.'

'I thought you were wrecked,' I said, disappointed at this tame ending.

'We were, later on,' he said. 'I 've got the log at home; you can see it if you like.'

The rest of that morning I spent drawing a group of golden brainstones around which variegated weed waved like heraldic mantlings. But while at work I found an increasing difficulty in keeping my feet, and I seemed to be thrown about without consciousness of any outside force. Then the weed and the soft corals appeared to sway more than usual, and even the fish were 'side-stepping' in an unusual way. I began to wonder if anything had gone wrong with the air-supply, but as I felt all right I continued with the job. Next time I looked up, the water had become murky and the visibility so reduced that there was no good in staying down longer.

'What's up?' I asked, when at the top of the ladder they had removed my helmet. 'Everything's going round down below, and it's thick as a London fog.'

'Reckon it's the wake of that tramp out there,' said Whitfield, pointing seawards.

That night he continued his story of the *Seabird*.

'Fill your glass and tell me where I was,' he said.

'You'd just arrived in Falmouth,' I replied, 'with your seams like a Venetian blind.'

'Well,' he said, 'we left Falmouth a week later, with a smoke screen belching from our engine-room. Do you know, the damn engine seized before we were past the Lizard, and what's more, do you know we were heartily glad of it, both of us. We'd had enough of machinery. What we wanted was to ruddy-well sail.

'First night out the wind was fair and fresh,' he continued, consulting his log, 'and we reduced our distance to Madeira considerably, but by noon of next day we were lying in a flat calm, and it wasn't till sunset that a breeze came up from the east. Then soon after dark we picked up Ushant Light, the wind freshened rapidly, and soon we were tearing along on a south-south-westerly course with our lee-rail under water. It was grand sailing. We could see ourselves crossing the bay in record time. It must have been about eight o'clock when I relieved Dunch at the tiller. There was some question of whether we should shorten sail, but the temptation to drive her was too strong. So I settled down and had four of the most wonderful hours of my life, almost standing on the lee-side of the cockpit with the tiller hard against my chest, and the old *Seabird* riding like a gull. I little guessed 'twas her swan song.

'As the night wore on, the wind strengthened until it was blowing a gale from the south-east. Several times I almost turned Dunch out to shorten sail. At midnight I daren't carry on any longer, so there was nothing for it but to down mainsail and heave to, under storm-jib and mizzen. All next day we lay hove to, and it blew a steady gale from south-east. The seas were tremendous and we shipped a few heavy ones. Then we decided to bring her more nearly head on by rigging the sea anchor. But no sooner done than the line carried away, leaving us wallowing again in the trough of the sea. We then slung the kedge on to the foot of the square-sail, and paid it out ahead with a bridle on the yard.

But it didn't help her much. After that the bumpkin shrouds carried away, so we lowered the sail and lashed it over the cockpit, where it did more good by keeping out the seas, which were breaking aboard all the time.

'Some time during the night our improvised sea anchor carried away. To add to our troubles, she was leaking again. By morning the water was six inches above the cabin floor. It was impossible to keep dry. Streams of water fell on us constantly as we lay in our bunks. Our eating, too, had been a bit sketchy, and I'd foolishly had breakfast from a tin of pork and beans left over from supper. That laid me out good and proper, some sort of ptomaine poisoning. All that day we lay while the gale still blew. I remember every second of it. Next morning a German steamer came close by and wanted to take us aboard. It took us the hell of a time to make them understand we didn't want to go.

'Soon after they had plunged away on their course the end of our main halyards went, and Dunch had to go aloft and fetch it down. I was too weak to be of much use. After midday the wind had gone round to south-west and had moderated, so Dunch got sail on her and off we went again. But the effort was short-lived. By four-thirty there was a gale from the south-west with a wicked cross-sea, and there was nothing to do but heave her to again, this time under foresail only. Blowed if it didn't blow clean out of the bolt ropes, with a report like a cannon. After that we could do nothing but let her lie; so Dunch got a primus going and we had some tea, well laced with rum. That reminds me, fill your glass.'

After a few moments' interlude to crack a bit of ice and consider our present comfortable situation, he went on:

'That next night was a mighty long one, and the day after there was still that gale from the south-west. 'Twas becoming monotonous, to say the least of it. It was disheartening, too, because all the time we were drifting steadily back, and the one thing we were determined on was not to turn and run for home. We had only a double-reefed trysail on her, and damned if the sheet of that didn't carry away during the afternoon. At this time I was lying in my bunk too ill to be of any use, but I remember it must have been about midnight when Dunch came below. He had hardly climbed into his bunk when there was a roar of rushing water, and the next thing I knew was that I was flat on my face against the ship's side, pressed down by a huge weight of solid water. I remember thinking calmly enough to myself: "So this is the end."

'Gradually she righted herself, but we were in bad shape, for she was half filled with water, and with every lurch it charged about. I don't know how I got back into my bunk, but I remember Dunch piling on the sodden blankets and greatcoats. I couldn't move an inch, and I can still feel their weight.

'Things were worse on deck, for the mizzen-mast had gone, the dinghy, skylights, fo'c'sle hatch, and parts of the bulwarks were washed away, in fact, the deck was completely cleared. Dunch then set to work to pump her out. But the pump kept choking. Each time he cleared the suction he had to go completely under water.

'Next morning the wind had eased a bit and Dunch got the trysail up, with the intention of trying to make for land. When he went to take the tiller he found that the rudder had gone. There was nothing for him to do but pump; and, as I lay in my bunk, I watched the water rush from side to side of the cabin, gradually demolishing everything. It broke out the drawers and lockers under me, and began to steal the covers off my bed. With each roll I felt the framework begin to give, and the cross-boards supporting the mattress were washing out, one by one. At this point Dunch logged, "Decided to abandon ship," but I wonder how he thought he was going to do it.'

I interrupted here to ask why there weren't more steamers on the route. 'Blown out of the course,' he replied; 'too far west and south for the steamer lines.'

But as it happened, a steamer, also blown out of her course, did come along; a Spaniard loaded down with coal, 'bucking her way slowly south, with green water coming over her fo'c'sle at almost every sea,' and somehow these unfortunate mariners were got on board. The final entries in the log speak for themselves.

10 a.m.   Pump jammed, unable to clear same. Commenced bailing out with bucket.

Noon.   Distress signal hoisted.
Decided to abandon ship, as she was in a semi-waterlogged condition, and Dunch was unable to keep the water under. Whitfield still laid up with diarrhoea and very weak.

2.30 p.m.   S.S. *Vasco* arrived, and sent boat to our assistance.
Sea cock opened and bilge suction-pipe holed before abandoning ship.

E. S. DUNCH.
E. WHITFIELD.

No sooner did these two lunatics reach England than they purchased another ship and, setting out again, reached Bermuda in safety.

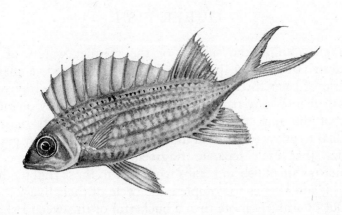

CHAPTER VII

QUEER FISH

FLOATING about the surface of the warmer waters of the western Atlantic are patches of sargassum weed, a marine prairie of over three million square miles. Coaxed by wind and drift into long parallel lines which stretch away on either side of the ship, these yellow sponge-like clusters must be familiar to every traveller in those seas. But how many people realize that each separate fragment provides a home for numerous small fish and crabs who trust to those frail tendrils, leaves, and berries to complete the cycle of their lives?

Out of scarcely more than a bucketful of this weed I shook at least two dozen fish, and ten times that number of crabs, shrimps, and worms. Most of the fish were the long, narrow pipe fish, closely related to the better-known sea-horse, but

without his arched back and curling tail.   One was a small
trigger fish, and two were slate-coloured midgets with a
bright silver patch on their bellies.   The most interesting of
all was the sargassum fish, who takes his name from the weed
he lives in and whose appearance he imitates so well.   His
disguise is as perfect as that of the little Indo-Pacific man-
grove fish, which can hardly be distinguished from the dead
leaves of that tree which float in the water, or of the young
fish described by Dr. Th. Mortensen, which, in the Bay of
Panama, swim among fragments of driftwood, and can so
simulate the appearance of the wood that even when they
are both taken and put into a dish of water together they
can scarcely be discerned apart.

Only by shaking the sargassum fish from the weed was it
possible to discover its presence, for the shape and markings
of the little creature blended so well with its surroundings
that the closest scrutiny failed to find it.

Transferred to the aquarium, it had the same stealthy habits
as the angler fish whom I had once seen capture its prey.

I remember, as in a nightmare, the sinister expression of that
yellow toad-like creature when, fixing its eye on a small fish
who had strayed too close to its domain, it had slowly stalked,

step by step on its flippers, over the rock. There was absolutely no emotion portrayed, but the manifest certainty of success was almost terrifying. The victim seemed hypnotized, and made no effort to move until its destroyer was close upon it. Then, as the angler lifted the rod which lay along its forehead and swept its tasselled end through the water, the little fish moved forward as if to inquire. Snap! Quicker than human eye could see, it was engulfed, and the same deadly expressionless stare of the angler told nothing. Only the twitchings of the sufferer inside its stomach betrayed the fact that the final act of the drama had been accomplished.

While on a dismal subject it might be as well to mention the great Moray eel, who in both the Atlantic and Pacific

Oceans grows to a length of eight or ten feet, and who lurks with mouth wide open in the crevices of the coral reefs, ready to snap its incurved, and poison-bearing, teeth on any unwitting visitor. In the Pacific this eel is a far greater danger to the pearl divers than sharks, with whom they can deal, for should a groping hand be caught inside those jaws there is little chance of release, and drowning must be the inevitable result. Only the strongest lungs can hold out till the grip is momentarily loosened, preparatory to a firmer hold. Only in that last half-second is there chance of escape.

There is also in all tropical and sub-tropical seas the voracious barracuda, in appearance akin to our freshwater pike, which may attain a length of eight feet, whose teeth are like scimitars and whose strike is like a flash. As long ago as the year 1665 the Sieur de Rochefort, in his *Natural History of the Antilles*, writes of this fish: 'Among the monsters greedy and desirous of human flesh, which are found on the coasts of the islands, the Becune is one of the most formidable. It is a fish which has the figure of a pike, and which grows to six or eight feet in length and has a girth in proportion. When it has perceived its prey, it launches itself in fury, like a bloodthirsty dog, at the men whom it has perceived in the water. Furthermore it is able to carry away a part of that which it has been able to catch, and its teeth have so much venom that its smallest bite becomes mortal if one does not have recourse at that very instant to some powerful remedy in order to abate and turn aside the force of the poison.' The description holds good to-day. Dr. Wood-Jones, F.R.S., in his *Coral and Atolls*, 1910, says: 'I have seen a Cocos native, the whole of whose calf muscles had been torn away by the cruel teeth of this large relation of the pike. The baracouta is an ugly and dangerous fish, for it is of all sea-creatures the most difficult to see, and it has a habit of dashing upon whatever stirs in the water.' Captain W. L. Wilson, a native of the Bahamas, has written: 'I knew of a case of a man who was walking quickly on a shallow reef beside deep water, and a barracuda flashed up and bit him on the foot. In this case, the cause, I think, was his white foot going in and out of the water quickly, for anything that moves quickly they will flash at. They give a ghastly bite.'

But these are rare acquaintances. I have never met a Moray eel except in an aquarium, and though I have seen a number of comparatively small barracuda, I never came across any of them when diving. I can assure people who contemplate these and other unpleasant eventualities from an arm-chair at home, that once they grow accustomed to being under water there is no greater apprehension of danger than there is when preparing to cross Piccadilly Circus.   There is certainly less actual danger to be met on the reefs than there is in motoring on the main roads of England.   Mountaineers have

told me that when climbing, the risks they run seem a paltry price for the exhilaration experienced.   So it is with diving. The importance of one's own entity fades to nil and any slight personal danger seems immaterial.

One of my chief surprises when under water was the apparent ease with which fish move.   The flight of birds is the only thing that approaches it.   In comparison, all the wayfarings of terrestrial creatures seem uncouth hobblings.

And as surprising as their ease of movement is their power of coming to a sudden halt. At one moment they will be swimming fast, at the next all forward movement has ceased. On land, where there is friction to overcome momentum, such precision is difficult to achieve; in a clear liquid it is all the more remarkable.

Fish, when drawn, are usually portrayed with all fins erect and all spines at 'the ready'; but this is entirely incorrect, for only when aggressive or frightened or displaying before the female do they appear in such a way. That part of the dorsal fin which is nearest the head, and which is generally armatured, is seldom raised, and the ventral and anal fins are only used for balance, so that the outstanding impression is one of streamlines from snout to end of tail.

Speaking of display, an interesting example of fish behaviour may often be seen on the reef, and even sometimes in the aquarium. Two blue-striped grunts, golden in colour, with markings of turquoise blue from head to tail, will suddenly come face to face, their mouths will flash open, showing scarlet interiors, and the two fish will remain, as it were staring each other down. It has been suggested that this is a form of intimidation, that each tries to frighten the other by a sudden exhibition of scarlet. Experiments have been carried out in which two of the species have been induced to rush at the same morsel of food. Instead of one or the other arriving first and getting away with it, as might be expected, both fish, on seeing each other, neglect the bait and demonstrate to each other with wide-open mouths. Lizards use the vivid red of their open mouths in a similar way for intimidation. Chameleons are known to bluff their enemies by gaping at them. Many snakes do the same when threatening.

But if we compare this behaviour with that of many birds, we see that it may, after all, arise from another emotion. Ceremonial gaping, as it has been called, is well known to ornithologists. J. G. Millais, describing the mating display of the red-breasted merganser, writes: 'With magnificent crest fully spread the drake turns his head, twisted at an angle of some sixty degrees to the water, towards the female, and opens his beak to its fullest extent, revealing the brilliant red interior.' E. A. Armstrong, writing of the common shag on our coasts, says: 'It is as certain as anything can be in these matters that the revelation of the yellow mouth has a stimulating or seductive effect on the bird which sees it.' Case after case might be cited of birds acting in this way to attract the opposite sex. It may then be that with the fish the action can fulfil either of two purposes, and that as with humans, in love or war, surprise is an important element of success. We must not imagine that one particular action can only arise from one particular cause. We ourselves can use a smile to express sympathy and disdain as well as mirth.

As a corollary to all this, one has only to sit in an hotel lounge and watch the contortions of the various people who use the writing-tables. Each individual has his own pantomime to perform before he can put pen to paper, or while he does so, and it would be a difficult task for an unknowing observer to correlate all these acrobatics as symptomatic of the same endeavour.

There is a pretty little fish of the Chaetodont family, commonly called the four-eye. It is so named because on each side, close to the base of its tail, it wears a large circular black-and-white mark which resembles an eye. But for all its daintiness it carries a formidable array of spines in the two fins which run most of the length of its body, above and below. In the ordinary way these lie close to the body, but when the fish is alarmed or attacked, up come these 'hackles' immediately. Added to this he swims backwards, and pretends that the black-and-white ocelli are really his eyes, and that his head is in the hinder region of his body. In that way he bamboozles his aggressor and slips into the safety of a nearby crevice.

Much the same device has been adopted by certain butter-flies which have been observed by Mortensen on the island of Tobago. He writes: 'As is well known, the species of this genus have some peculiar thin prolongations from the hind-wings, sometimes only small and inconspicuous, but in most species, especially the larger tropical forms, long and threadlike. There may be one, two, or three pairs of such prolongations, of different length, the lower or the middle pair being generally much the longest. In most species there is a conspicuous coloured spot on the underside of the hind-wings at the base of the processes; sometimes there are two such spots. These butterflies, when resting, always close their wings, so that only the underside is seen. Then they have the remarkable habit of moving the hind-wings alter-nately up and down, whereby the threadlike prolongations are kept in constant movement, looking perfectly like antennae. The conspicuous coloured spot at the base of the pseudo-antennae perfectly suggests an eye—and thus the impression is produced that this end is the head, the real antennae being held quite motionless, and the real head being black and quite inconspicuous. . . . So vivid is the impression, in the more perfect species, that although I knew it all perfectly well and had observed it many times, I had always the in-voluntary impression that the tail end was the head, and, of course, persons with no special knowledge of insects would invariably take this to be the head.'

In England many of the hairstreak butterflies, which belong to the same family, have similar appendages, and if we are lucky enough to observe the handsome swallow-tail butterfly, now confined to the fens of Norfolk and Cambridgeshire, we can well imagine that the special development of the wing which gives the owner its name, coupled with the bright eye-like markings close below it, might very easily delude an enemy who had not by repeated experience learned what to expect.

Another interesting method of self-defence, on the reefs, is

shown by the porcupine fish. The scales of this fish have
been transformed into spines, and the belly, like that of the
allied puffer fishes, has a skin that is capable of great disten-
sion. By drawing in air or water the fish can swell itself
into a sphere, from whose taut hide the spines then protrude
at right angles. In that condition it is too formidable a
mouthful for any ordinary pursuer. So effective, indeed, is
this armour as a protection that in some of the Pacific islands
the natives, at one time, used the dried skins of the fish to
make war-helmets, and many of the illustrations in early
accounts of the Gilbert, the Marshall, and the Kingsmill
islands show such armour in use.

Louis L. Mowbray, the director of the Bermuda Govern-
ment Aquarium, is a mine of information on all that concerns
the reefs. Of the Chaetodonts mentioned above, he told me
how he had often seen them enter the mouth of a Moray
eel, or of one of the bigger rockfish, and proceed to clear
away the parasites which had accumulated there. He said
that the larger fish never attempted to take advantage of their
scavenging visitor, but that they seemed only too willing to
have their toilet completed in this way. Similarly, that parrot
fish may often be seen balancing upright in the water while
smaller fish of the Wrasse family clean their scales of coral
debris. This reminded me of crocodiles who allow the
'crocodile-bird' to enter their open mouths and remain there
unharmed while it picks leeches and other parasites from
their jaws.

When we were discussing colour change he pointed out a
yellow coney or sea bass which, though normally of a canary
colour all over, invariably changes to dark brown when put
into an aquarium. This particular fish had behaved in that
way when first caught, and for some time afterwards. But
one day there was introduced into the tank a magnificent
golden grouper which Mr. Vincent Astor had brought with
him from the Galapagos Islands. The moment that the coney
saw this resplendent creature it forgot its own sulky humours
and flashed out into its brightest tints, as if in an effort to
outshine the new arrival. Since then, whether from male

rivalry or merely from the force of good example, it has never changed back to the more sombre hue.

This aquarium has probably the finest collection of tropical fish in the world. This is, in a large measure, due to the generosity of Vincent Astor, whose yacht the *Nourmahal* is fitted out with special tanks for transporting live specimens from the South Seas, the Cocos Islands, the Galapagos, or wherever else there are species to be collected. And there can be few people alive who know better how to maintain these captives in health than Mowbray himself. 'Born on the reef,' he understands the psychology of his charges, and—

E

nearly as important from my point of view—he understands
the psychology of visitors. From the first moment that I
met him I was given the freedom of the tanks, and anything
I wanted to draw was moved to a special aquarium in his

own studio. Many of the more elusive fish who had escaped
our traps were drawn in this way; for, needless to say, during
the fifteen or twenty minutes below the surface at any one
place it was impossible to do more than hint at the general
character of the passers-by. Indeed, it was a most tantalizing

experience to stand there amid that wealth of interest and
know that one's greatest efforts could convey scarcely more
suggestion of the truth than a trouser button does of the
garment to which it belongs.

But there are other things of interest beside coral and fish.
One may, for instance, find the large conch shells which,
with the tips filed off, serve as trumpets all over Polynesia
and the West Indies. In Polynesia they are used by the
natives to signal to each other on the reef at night. In
Bermuda it is the vendors of fish who sound them to adver-
tise their approach. In the crevices of the coral and in the
reef-floor will be seen sea-urchins whose blue spines are ten
and twelve inches long. Those spines are sharp and will
easily pierce the flesh. They are brittle, too, and break off
easily. A small fragment under the skin can produce a nasty
sore. Starfish, some compact and scarlet, others with thin

brown feathery fronds, are conspicuous on the reef. And
there is always the weed, some of which covers the dead coral
with the richest moss, while other forms wave in the ocean

swells like banners in the wind. Drawing can but hint at the shapes. Nothing can express the movement. Unlike cornfields, whose ripening heads bend all together to the same breeze, neighbouring clumps of weed, swayed by opposing currents, change and counterchange their direction, achieving a rhythm more subtle than the choreography of any ballet.

CHAPTER VIII

COOPER'S ISLAND

It has been said that Bermuda consists of several hundred bridges connected by excrescences of coral rock; that on the rock grow cedar-trees and tourists; that the trees are stunted and the tourists are intoxicated. That description may be unkind and exaggerated; nevertheless, there is a modicum of truth in it. Islands abound and so do bridges, but the former are in the majority, so that it is still possible to find patches of land on which the cedar-trees flourish and where there are no inhabitants.

On one of these, called Cooper's Island, at the south-eastern extremity of the group, I landed one morning and spent two days entirely alone. Like its neighbours, this island has seen stirring events since Juan de Bermudez first landed on it in 1510. The famous Captain Tew sailed from there on that eventful voyage when he turned pirate, and became so successful in his new role that before settling down in Madagascar he was able to distribute £3,000 to each member of his gallant crew, whose watchword had been 'A golden chain or a wooden leg.' Other buccaneers, known and un-known, have landed on these shores, and tales of buried treasure have become a commonplace, but there are also tales of evil spirits and demons who guard the treasure, and 'Fire drakes who rise out of the ground and assend the aire and have been seen to fly over that portion of the island where the treasure was buried,' so that no part of it has ever yet been recovered, save only a few coins and some silver spoons.

In the year 1690, however, there was granted to one Thomas Neale a royal charter for the recovering of treasure which was reputed to have been buried by crews of wrecked ships before ever 'The Burmudaes' were settled, and in order to facilitate the carrying out of this project, statements were taken from important local residents. The following is typical:

The Deposition of Mr. Joseph Ming of Cooper's Island, being the south-east point of the Island of Bermuda, who deposeth and sayth: 'That there hath been ever since his time a great discourse in these Islands, by the antient Inhabitants, that a great treasure hath been hid in this said Cooper's Island, and likewise that the marks and signe of it were three yallow wood trees, that stood tryangular, upon one of w'ch was a plate of brass nailed, and on the other were severall names or letters cutt thereon, and that this depon't with some others to his assistance did about two years since endeavour to discover this treasure by digging in a peece of ground lying in the center of this tryangle of trees, for five or six dayes, but mett with noe success therein, soe grew soe tired and left off, not being able nor willing to bestowe any longer time or paines therein, although the ground was very easye to digg, and that the place they digged was foure or five yards square. . . . And this depon't further sayth that his grandfather had an extraordinary confidence of finding great treasures here from the satisfaction of the tradition and markes here found, upon which about sixty yeares since this depon'ts grandfather went for England and made his application to the proprietors to purchase this said Coopers Island and carried with him a considerable quantity of Ambergreece and presented the proprietors with a good part thereof, upon which the proprietors offered him Davids Island in lieu of his present which consists of tenn times more land and intrinsick value then this Coopers Island, which he rather chose than the said Davids Island for the hopes he had as aforesaid, and likewise oblidged himselfe to the proprietors to mantaine seven men continually at his owne charge towards manning the forts of the said Islands.

'JOSEPH MING.'

It has recently been suggested that the inscription on the brass plate was probably written in Latin or Spanish, which would not have been understood, and that, in any case, it was nothing more than a record of a previous landing or a claim to the island. This seems much more reasonable than to suppose that, having buried vast treasure, the owners would immediately put up signs and marks to tell all new arrivals where it lay. A similar fable exists in the Cocos Islands where, even to-day, intelligent men hazard their lives and health in following imaginary clues derived from the scratchings of bored or drunken sailors.

It was good to be alone, and to know that in whatever direction I cared to look there would be no sight or sound to remind me of humanity. Nothing but the bo'sun bird reflecting the emerald green of the sea from its breast and imitating the cry of the sirens as it circled overhead.

On this island, where I found myself voluntarily marooned, there was neither science nor art, but there was warm sand, and sun with a cooling breeze, and shady groves of sweet-smelling trees. As I wandered along the shore I thought of the three Crusoes who had been the first settlers on the island and who 'began their common wealth for a while with equall and brotherly regencye,' until making 'a priuye search into euery nooke and corner of the craggie rocks for whatsoeuer of value the open armed ocean had for a long time conuayed thether and secretly horded up, so that at length (answerable to their wish and paines) they chaunced vpon the good-lyest and greatest peece of Amber-Grece that the world is knowen euer yet to have had in one lumpe.'

I thought, too, of the crew of the whaling steamer *Morote* who, in 1928, had captured a whale that contained two hundred and forty-eight pounds of ambergris, valued at £13,200. But in my wanderings I found no trace of that greasy and heavy-smelling substance so highly esteemed by man and so gladly ejected by the whale. Once only did I anticipate treasure, when I came upon the flat trail of a turtle and thought to follow it to a goodly store of eggs; but it merely led me across a narrow isthmus of sand and then disappeared in the sea beyond. I therefore consoled myself with reflection on the fate of the three men who found the ambergris and who became rich folk; 'and so to be proude, and from being proude to be ambitious, and from that into a contempt one for another, and a desire of super-eminencye: so that lastly (being only three forlorne men in a narrowe desolate place, three thousand miles from their natiue country and to their knowledge in noe likly-hoode of euer recoueringe of it) they fell into a most hott and violent contention for superioritye and commande; so that quickly they came from wordes to blowes. . . . And thus in this desolate place and miserable fashion liued thes three poore men . . . so that their cloathes were all worne and falne away from their backs, and their hopes of forrainge reliefe as naked as their bodyes.'

Noon changed to afternoon and sunset gave way to moon-light like the changing colours of a rockfish. As the golden glow faded in the west the light of the rising moon grew stronger, and for a moment each of the two luminaries cast a shadow on opposite sides of where I stood. Gradually the moon took over command. The night temperature was perfect. I lay on the naked sands and watched the shore grow wider and wider as all dunes and hillocks disappeared in the moonlight, and there was left only a flat world bounded by a sea of silver. When I woke after a few hours' sleep, the moon had passed across the zenith and the western sky again held court, but, before that fading light had given the stars one brief hour in which to kindle, a faint grey streak on the eastern horizon proclaimed that the sun was again at hand. One by one the stars dimmed out, dove-grey clouds took clearer form as their edges were tinged with ivory; the eastern sky grew warmer and the wide acres of sand diminished in area. Only the morning star was still shining. Then the sky was touched with fire and wild streaks of light flashed up behind the purple clouds, the last star disappeared, and suddenly the east was aflame.

Back on the main island there was excitement among the scientists, for it was the night after the full moon, and that is the time each month when the reproductive segments of a phosphorescent worm called the palolo come to the surface to breed. Fifty minutes after sunset is the marriage hour and, on this occasion, shortly before that time, an aged professor armed with a silk net and an iron bucket, accompanied by a middle-aged lady, were seen to embark in a light skiff and pull their craft into the bay. Then as darkness fell we could hear excited cries from the boat. 'There's one, a female,' called the old man, 'and there's the male on the right. Watch! Watch, there they go! WATCH!'

'A perfect copulation,' said the lady.

From the shore we could now see, dotted like stars in the water, the bright circling lights given out by the females as they rose to the surface. A few seconds after each appearance the lesser glow of a male would be visible, then almost instantly it would be seen rushing towards the other, and after a few seconds of intensified luminosity, the light of both would fade out as they sank together to the bottom.

Different species of the palolo are known in many parts of the world, and in all cases they have a similar regularity of habit, so much so that in the Trobriand Islands the date of an annual feast, associated with the return of ancestral spirits to the village, is determined by the appearance of the palolo.

In Samoa and Fiji their appearances constitute important fixed dates in the calendar, and events are reckoned as so long before or after the time of swarming. In both these groups of islands the worm appears in very much larger quantities than in the Atlantic, and it is considered such a delicacy that chiefs on the coast send baskets of it as presents to their neighbours inland. When cooked it is said to have the appearance of spinach and to taste and smell something like fresh fish's roe. Only on two days in October and November does it appear, and the dates are looked forward to with eagerness by men, women, and children, who are ready to rush into the water and scoop the assembled millions into baskets of coco-nut fibre. In the Gilbert Islands, farther to the west, where the worm is known as 'the glistener,' the swarms appear in June and July; in the Malay Straits a similar species emerges in March and April on the second and third nights after full moon, while in Japan their relatives come to the surface at a corresponding time in October and November.

Comdr. William Burrows, R.N., writing in *Nature*, describes one of these events. He says: 'To attend a "rising" is an unforgettable event. . . . I have boarded my canoe at 04.30 after a sleep in the village and paddled out to a position about half-way out to the main reef, which skirts the shore at this spot at a distance of about a mile. Then torches were shone into the water vertically from the boat's side to see if there are any indications. If it is the right day small stray bits of the worm make their appearance and nets are got ready. Then, when the first light of dawn appears, great funnels of worms burst to the surface and spread out until the whole area is a wriggling mass of them, brown and green in colour. . . . The worms also provide an annual feast for the fish; for all around and between the boats big fish and sharks cruise quietly along, gulping them in, and take no notice whatever of the boats or their occupants.'

But these worms are not the only examples that we know of lunar periodicity in reproduction. The oyster and the queen scallop spawn at the full moon, and the great shoals of herring come under the same influence. Many other instances might be given, up to and including the human race. I would even hazard a guess that the well-known romantic effect of moonlight on humans may have a deeper significance than many of us imagine.

As we watched from the shore at Bermuda and saw the last pair of lights flicker and fade, there came to our ears from across the water the sound of singing and the music of banjo and concertina, and a few minutes later two motor launches filled with jubilant negroes passed down the channel.

'Warm work in town to-night,' said a white man on the pier.

'Well,' replied his coloured neighbour, 'if dey win cricket match and bring back d' cup, ah reckon they got perfect right misbehave themselves little bit.'

'Cricket, indeed,' said a ghost at my elbow, and I thought of two old newspapers I 'd seen a few days previously:

'*April* 12*th*, 1788. To be sold by Public Vendue, on Thursday the 17th day of April, at Two o'clock in the afternoon. . . . The Personal Estate of the late Benj. Tibby consisting of House Furniture, 1 Negro man, 2 ditto Women, 3 ditto Boys, and 2 ditto Girls.'

'*Jan.* 9, 1790. To be sold. A healthy young Negro Wench, fit for the house or plantation; she can wash, starch, iron, cook and sew. Salt will be taken in payment.'

CHAPTER IX

EAST OF SUEZ

ONE fine day in the spring of 1938 I found myself travelling from Paris to Marseilles *en route* for the Red Sea. In the valleys through which we passed acres and acres of blossoming fruit-trees shone purple in the sun. Beyond them the grey, vine-terraced hills recalled the purple of the 'Emperor of Wines,' as George Meredith called Burgundy. From Dijon to Lyons one skirts, on the right, the whole Burgundian wine-field. The names of the stations and the villages through which one passes read like a wine-list: Chambertin, Musigny, Vougeot, Nuits-Saint-Georges, Aloxe Corton, Beaune, Pommard, Volnay, Mersault, Puligny, Santenay. It is surprising that all these famous vineyards can be within the short distance of forty miles. Still more surprising that several of the most illustrious names on that list represent no greater extent of land than that of an English small holding. Musigny covers but twenty-four acres. The soil of vineyards needs hundreds of years of devoted and intelligent care before it will give of its best. Age makes the vineyard, as it also makes the wine, but, for the former, it must be reckoned in centuries. Tradition says that on one plot at Musigny the soil is considered so precious that the workers on leaving their estate will scrape the earth from their sabots before crossing the boundary.

We reached Marseilles, we reached the ship, and eventually we sailed.

Next morning we awoke to a 'stark oil calm,' through which we ploughed with an almost indecent disrespect. Most of the passengers had come round by long sea. There were two nuns with eyes cast down. There were two hot-gospellers with eyes cast up. There were Indian women, Scots engineers, Australians. The hot-gospellers saw celestial cities in the clouds, the bo'sun saw dirty weather. The latter was right, and we had a bit of a blow which levelled both the saved and the unsaved.

I was glad to get off that ship, the first I 've ever been on

without a soul. She had less of that commodity than a
Channel steamer, and I seem to remember nothing more of
her and her passengers than a jazz pattern of gramophones,
beach pyjamas, gin, dice, and vaccination notices. Oh, yes,
there was a girl who sang 'Don't love a dog, have a baby,'
and there was another who confided to me the tale of her
shattered romance. It seems that she saw him first from a
stage box, that he was tall and slight, that his dark hair waved
and that 'he played *divinely*.' She had leaned from her box
when he played *Moonshine* and their eyes had met when he
played *We Two*, and when the curtain fell he had sent her
a bouquet: 'To the girl in the box with the beautiful eyes.
Would she dine next night?' And she did, and he talked
about his art and himself, and about himself and his art, so
that her heart went out to him, and she asked *what* was his
greatest ambition. Then he had said that 'he thought—that
it probably—was—to keep a pub.'[1]

A few hours were spent in Port Said denying solicitous
shoeblacks and refusing importunate vendors of postcards,
and then the train rolled out across the isthmus, showing on
the one side the dull walls of proud man's little canal and on
the other side a panorama of time-worn customs and age-
old history; mud walls, minarets, pink sands, splay-legged
camels, black-cloaked women in lush green fields, palms,
sheep, goats, water-wheels, vultures, and ophthalmia. I
arrived in Suez a quarter of an hour too late to catch the
oil tanker which would have dropped me at my destination.
The next two days were occupied, for the most part, in
trying to get a passage on some local trading steamer, but
there was time to wander about the town or sit at a café
and contemplate life in general.

[1] Note: About a year after the publication of the first edition of this
book I had a letter from Paris. It was from my confidante on the ship.
She wrote: 'You have robbed me of an important item in my repertoire.
Last night I told that story to some friends in a café and a Russian artist
among them said, "Varee amusing but it is not true. You read that in
a book on feeshes by a man with a beard."' She added that now nobody
would believe her. So the usual process is reversed and fact becomes
fiction.

One of the charms of travelling is that apart from the stimulus of an ever-changing scene, and apart from the joy of 'escape,' we are able to view the world with the irresponsibility of children, unthinking and ignorant of the drama which lies behind each and every façade, whether it be the forbidding features of some gaunt factory or the painted face of some unhappy wife.

Psychologists tell us that we are all compounded of the male and female elements in varying proportions, and that even in the most blood-curdling dictator there can be found traces of the gentler sex, just as in the most tender-hearted mother there will sometimes be seen glimpses of the he-man. The artist in particular, we are told, combines the attributes of both sexes. He is at one moment passive and receptive as only a female can be; at the next he is forceful and thrusting, as the male in his ecstasy. But only from the former can the latter be born. With hopes, then, of ultimately completing the cycle, I sat and absorbed the varying colours of the cosmopolitan procession which passed before me: Egyptians, Arabs, Nubians, Italians, Greeks; tarbush, turban, trilby hat. Sheep led through the town by a small boy, who enticed them forward with a handful of beans, reminded me of public and politicians at home. A fellah with goatskin water-bottle called his trade through the street. A donkey with zigzag patterns cut like a garter in the hair of each fore-shoulder was driven by a boy in an orange shirt. Last but not least, an Arab woman who, when passing, smiled and lifted a corner of her veil, revealing for a moment a blue tattoo mark on her lower lip.

Thanks to the local manager of the Shell Oil Company, I eventually found myself on board a small tanker. The ship, like others of its kind, had a deep draught but little freeboard. The smallest waves washed on board. 'Tankers are like pigs in the water,' said the captain. 'They 've no life in them.' I shared a cabin with an oil-driller from Texas. His pride was in a brand-new pair of riding boots. When he undressed for bed his breeches and jacket were thrown on the floor, but the boots were laid tenderly on the settee.

Twenty-four hours' steaming down the Gulf of Suez brought us to Towila, a truly desert island. Over its whole area I saw no more herbage than would fit on a doormat. We arrived there soon after midday, and while some German and Egyptian oil surveyors were being put ashore with their gear I had an hour to spend ashore.

To my surprise the crusted sand which covered the whole surface of the island was filled with shells and dead coral. It was impossible to move without stepping on one or the other; in fact, the island seemed entirely composed of these materials. This was my first experience of real desert, of dry, parched, sterile soil, on which, all day and every day, the sun beats wantonly down as if trying to set on fire that which has already been burnt out. Distances were deceptive, and far-away objects seemed nearer than they afterwards turned out to be. A blue shimmering light on the horizon suggested water, and it was easy to imagine some unfortunate traveller pursuing this chimera hither and thither in vain hope.

Wading near the shore, I almost trod on a yellow skate or ray. His triangular head was more lemon-coloured than the rest of his flat body, and as he glided along by gentle undulations of the lateral fins, he was scarcely perceptible against the striated tide-marks in the sand. I followed closely for some twenty yards, and he seemed to be completely unaware of my presence. Not until I was within three feet of him did he give a sudden flick of his tail and, under cover of the

sediment thereby stirred up, quickly change direction and
shoot off at right angles. I followed him again and he
repeated the manœuvre rather more quickly, but before I
could catch up for a third time he had disappeared from view.

There are many varieties of these fish, from the well-known
skate of our own shores to the tropical manta who may
measure twenty feet across its body and weigh anything up
to five thousand pounds. These larger fish have a habit of
leaping from the water and falling back, flat on to the surface, so that the noise of their impact is like the crack of
thunder. In spite of their horned and terrifying appearance

they are not considered to have anything worse than a sulky nature, and seldom do harm to man unless attacked. Even then their behaviour is not vicious, for given the chance they will dive to the bottom and remain there motionless until their harpooner has grown weary and cut the line. The smaller rays are, in reality, much more to be feared; for, in some species, at the end of their whip-like tail or, in others, under one of the caudal fins, they carry a poisonous spine which can inflict a most grievous wound.

As I retraced my steps to land I noticed about fifteen rose-coloured crabs that had formed up in a semicircle on the edge of the water and were gradually converging on some hidden object. Before I reached them they had obviously cornered their quarry, and when eventually they dispersed at my near approach they left behind them the half-eaten pink body of an eel.

Wandering inshore, I was greeted by a sea-hawk which rose from a cairn-like elevation on the highest point of the island. Its mewing cries were at one moment pathetic and at the next threatening, and when I came closer and it was joined by its mate I realized that I was approaching their nest. I have since learned that for many generations this one spot has been the nesting-place of these birds, and that the elevation of the site is due entirely to the annual incre-ment of nesting material and offal which they collect. As I struck back towards the ship a solitary grey owl rose from under a stone and winged its way into the dusk.

During the evening a sandstorm blew up. Visibility was nil; a London fog couldn't have been more obliterative. Fortunately, we were at anchor far away from shipping routes. We had sand in the eyes, sand in the ears, sand in the mouth. We licked our fingers and wiped the dust off our eyelashes. Inside our shirts the grit collected and chafed our skin. But at dawn the sky was clear. As we picked our course through the reefs the island of Shadwan lay like a feather from a dove's breast on a mirror-like sea, while Sinai with its peaks, its crevasses, and its legends lay behind us, shining silver in the morning light.

F

Dr. Cyril Crossland, director of the research station to which I was travelling, has described how after such a sandstorm rain may fall. It his book, *Desert and Water Gardens of the Red Sea*, he writes: 'After the dust may come a furious squall of rain. Here, where rain is so visibly the coming of life to the earth, it is fitly heralded by the full majesty of vast cloud mountains with snowy summits, from whose dark bases issue continuous lightnings and thunder. In such weather heavy squalls may be expected from any quarter, causing much anxiety to sailors used to the regular winds of the Red Sea. One cloud mass may grow until the sky is covered, mountains hidden in a black veil of rain, a furious wind hiding the shore by a great brown cloud of dust. Before the squall reaches the vessel sail is reduced to a mere corner of the great triangle usually spread, amid much excited shouting. Lightning and thunder become almost continuous and the sea is lashed white with rain and spray. It is as cold and dark as night, and impossible to see more than a few yards ahead, all idea of entering harbour is given up, and a look out is kept *downwards* in case the vessel may pass over a shoal (which would be visible five fathoms down, in the clear water) on which she could anchor till the storm passed off. Suddenly a tiny rift appears in the cloud mass ahead; a mountain-top becomes visible through the rain, then the masts of a vessel in harbour. In five minutes we may have passed from darkness, storm, and anxious peering through rain, to the bright sunshine and calm of a summer sea.'

Speaking of navigation through the uncharted reefs that fringe the coast, the same author tells us: 'There is, indeed, no immediate necessity for aids to navigation, for the breeze, fresh but not strong, ripples the water so that the reefs shew among the blue-green of the deeper channels as clearly as the white squares of a chess board. . . . All those colours of shoaling sand and coral beds are only visible when the water is rippled. . . . Calm is thus more dangerous to a steamer than storm. . . . Sailing vessels are safe, as whenever they are under way the water is rippled and the reefs easily seen.'

CHAPTER X

GHARDAQA

THE port of Hurghada consists of a pier and a line of mud-walled houses, following the crescent of the bay. Behind them lies the desert, and from that, at a distance of some twenty miles, rise the mountains which form the western battlements of the Great Rift Valley, and which divide the Red Sea from the river Nile.

On the shore, close to the landing-stage, were lying a few canoes, and moored near by were native sailing feluccas. A ten-inch oil-pipe hung its nozzle over the pier, guttering its filthy dregs into the clean water.

I was met by Dr. Crossland. With his first words he directed my attention to some crimson and bronze alcyonaria, or soft corals, which grew on the girders of the pier. Like rich rosettes of royal velvet, they decorated the rusting iron, transforming the unromantic metal stanchions into pillars that would grace a palace. These growths, fleshy and leathery when contracted, as in the illustration (page 79), open out into bunches of exquisite daisy-like forms, each pin-head nodule expanding into a star-like bloom at the end of a long and delicate stalk. The change is as great as that of a full-blown rose from its earliest bud, but instead of happening once only in a season, it is of daily occurrence. On the Great Barrier Reef of Australia, and on many islands in the Pacific, allied species, yellow, verdigris-green, and lilac, grow abundantly, and Saville Kent has recorded a single colony

75

which spread over an area between fifty and sixty feet in diameter.

The marine research station at Ghardaqa, about seven miles from our port of entry, is a branch of the University of Egypt, and was planned and built by Dr. Crossland. For the study of corals no one could ask a better site, for the reefs are in full bloom within a hundred yards of the shore. There are no show aquariums, but the laboratories are close to the sea, and the observation tanks are filled with running water, which is fed through porcelain pipes lest any trace of metal should contaminate the supply. By skilful arrangement of windows there is a constant circulation of air through the rooms, so that even in midsummer the temperature is never oppressive.

Before I had been ashore more than a few hours the director suggested that we should experiment with the diving apparatus, for though the helmet had been among the first purchases of equipment for the station no one had hitherto made use of it. It was a different pattern to the one that I had used in Bermuda, being made of galvanized iron instead of copper, and having its window set at an angle so that the line of vision was thrown slightly downwards. This was, no doubt, excellent for collecting specimens, but not so good for drawing, as in order to see the full height of the coral which towered above me it was necessary to lean back to an extent almost dangerous to the balance. One of the essential things to remember in the use of this apparatus is that of maintaining the body in a vertical position. Should, by chance, the helmet be tilted forward or backward at more than a certain angle, the air within will escape, the metal casque will drop to the bottom, and the diver will arrive feet first at the surface.

Once again, as at Bermuda, the adjustment of weights took time. When I first stepped off the ladder, a few feet below the surface, I remained suspended at that depth, moving neither up nor down. It was necessary, therefore, to return for more weight. But lead was a scarce commodity in the desert, and communications with the outside world were slow. The only metal available was iron chain, and from a dozen yards of this we made a waist-belt that could be hooked or unhooked with ease. It is highly important that these extra weights should be detachable at a moment's notice. Should an emergency arise, there must be no hindrance to a speedy ascent.

At my next attempt to get below there was sufficient weight to keep *me* down, but not enough to overcome the buoyancy of the air-filled helmet as well. Before I reached the bottom I had nearly dropped out of my headgear. Once again the ladder had to be climbed, and this time they added to my breastplate some seven pounds' weight of spare parts from the launch's engine. This achieved for me perfection of equilibrium, and so my mind was free for the work in hand.

In Bermuda the sharks had an enviable reputation for altruistic behaviour, and the diving had been a comparatively casual affair, with no more hint of danger than in a children's nursery, but here in the Red Sea it was different. El Rayis, the captain of the launch, had had personal experience of them. He was fishing one day, standing waist-deep in water, when a shark came along, seized him by both legs, and carried him off his feet. Knowing the habits of sharks, he held his breath until the first rush was over and allowed himself to be carried along. Then, doubling himself up, he drove a finger and thumb into the animal's nostrils. A shark is a cowardly creature, and this time it was sufficiently frightened to let its victim go. El Rayis came to the surface, where he was rescued by his friends. But it was several months before he recovered from the attack, and he still carries deep scars on his legs, which I myself have seen and which testify to the truth of his story. In spite of such an experience he has nothing but scorn for these monsters, and does not hesitate to jump on the back of any one of them that may come prowling too near the launch.

But whatever El Rayis might feel about himself in this connection, he did not disguise his opinion that all white men were proverbially helpless in the water and that it was part of his job to look after them. Therefore, whenever

I prepared to descend he also got ready for his duties, divesting himself of his flowing robes and taking his place on the gunwale, ready to plunge in at a moment's notice.

As things turned out there was never any need for him to come to my assistance, for I didn't see a shark at any time when under water. Nevertheless, there were moments down below when, remembering the conversations I had heard in the local camp, I was glad to know that I had a guardian up aloft.

'Ever seen 'em in Shark Bay, other side of the point?' asked a superintendent of oil works. 'By jingo, you see 'em thick enough over there. Me go down? Not on your life. No future in that!'

'My word, they come like lightning!' said an Australian. 'Now if you escape the first rush you must walk towards them.' Then he went on to describe how I should let air out of the helmet to frighten them, or throw my sheet of white xylonite in such a way that they would see it and follow it. 'They always go for anything white that flickers in the water, soles of the feet or china plates—all the same thing. Natives of the Loyalty Islands in the South Seas always tie something dark over the soles of their feet when swimming in deep water.' He'd saved a man's life once by chucking plates into the sea, each one a little farther from the diver, and so gradually attracting the shark away till the man had time to come to the surface. He knew, too, of a deep-sea diver who, just as he was going down, saw a large shark awaiting him.

'What did he do? Why, he dropped a stick of dynamite overboard with a time-fuse attached. The shark made a grab and swallowed it, and I reckon, in twenty years you couldn't count the bits of that fish that came to the surface.'

The Arabs on this coast are entirely at home both in and on the sea. When, for instance, they wanted to move one of the anchors of the launch to steady the vessel for my operations, they would dive from the surface, pick up the anchor, and run with it under water. Then, dropping it at what they considered a better spot, they would return to the surface, showing no sign of unusual effort. Crossland describes how they may be seen in their little dug-out canoes, 'tearing along under full sail, the steersman busy throwing out the water with his spare hand, while the other occupant hangs to the mast which threatens to be carried away by the wind at every moment, and leans as far over the side as he can to prevent her capsizing.'

CHAPTER XI

DOWN BELOW

THE Red Sea district is generally pictured in the mind as a roasting wilderness where men's eyes burn in their sockets and their tongues cleave to the roofs of their mouths. But when I was there in April the temperature was scarcely higher than on a summer's day in England, and the nights were cool enough to make two blankets a necessity for comfortable sleep.

The sea is, of course, no more red than the Mediterranean Sea or the Atlantic or Pacific Oceans, but it has probably got its name from the colour of the mountains which run parallel to the coast on either side. Possibly the soil, which after heavy rain is carried down from those same hills and discolours the water far out from the shore, may have had something to do with the title, or even the small berries, or sea pods, which at times may be seen floating in large drifts, making the water quite red in appearance.

The water itself was cooler than I expected, and the deeper I went the colder it became. Even in my descent of a few fathoms I could notice at least three distinct changes of temperature. No wonder, then, that corals which only thrive in warm water cannot exist at depths where the more genial surface currents never penetrate. Twenty minutes was the maximum time that I could spend below without chill. But what crowded moments those were! While in Bermuda the different forms of coral seemed hardly more than could be counted on the fingers of one hand, but here in every direction were new varieties. Crossland told me that, in one spot, he had counted twenty different species. If he had said twice or three times that number I should still have thought he was suffering from scientific reticence, for to me every square foot was unlike the next. He could see resemblances where I saw none, and where I thought I recognized two brothers he showed me that the Eskimos and Patagonians were hardly less related.

Besides the multitudinous hard corals which branched around me there were the alcyonaria, whose delicate tasselled heads formed bell-like flowers as they opened and closed in their search for food. Some of them were biscuit-coloured, others were every shade of lilac, some were rich and lustrous like those growing on the pier at Hurghada, others seemed fragile as thistledown.

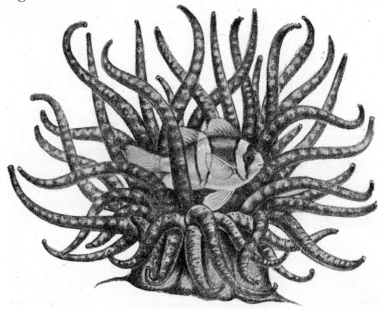

In among the crevices of the dead coral were giant ane-mones, among whose tentacles might be discovered a small fish marked with conspicuous white bars across its bronze body, which, either by long habit or by 'gentleman's agree-ment,' had gained immunity from the stinging cells of its host. Living as it does under cover of such a battery, it achieves a greater security from its enemies than it would have if dependent on its own resources. In order to repay the hospitality granted, it makes it its business to dart from cover and endeavour to lure or drive any passing stranger within reach of the tentacles. Should it be successful there is no lack of reward in the crumbs that fall from its host's table. Saville Kent records two other fish of this same family, and also a prawn, who live in this commensal way with other species of giant anemones on the Great Barrier Reef of Australia. Another parallel is to be found in the Portuguese man-of-war, a jelly-fish inhabiting the warmer waters of the

Atlantic Ocean, and taking its name from its sail, a gas-filled float, that projects above the surface of the water. Its long tentacles, sometimes stretching downward to a depth of fifty feet, can capture fish up to six inches in length, paralysing them by their stinging cells. But again there is a fish that has achieved immunity, and several of them may be found in the company of one host, darting among the tentacles for safety when pursued by larger fish.

T. C. Roughley tells of a hermit crab who, notwithstanding the protection afforded by a borrowed shell, likes to have one

or two of the smaller stinging anemones attached to the same covering, as if to make assurance doubly sure. Yet again, there is a crab in the Indian Ocean who carries stinging anemones about with him on his claws, brandishing these when attacked. In both these cases any defensive duties carried out by the anemone are well repaid by the crab, who not only constantly carries his companion to pastures new, but also, being a dirty feeder, provides it with a rich diet of scraps from his own meals. Neither last nor least in the long list of these marine partnerships is the well-known naucrates, the little fish who always swims ahead of the shark and pilots him to his prey, knowing full well that there will be sufficient over from the meal to satisfy his own modest needs, added to which he will obtain security from the presence of the shark, who would certainly scare away any other predacious fish. Dr. Meyen in his *Reise um die Erde*, quoted by A. C. J. G. Günther, writes: 'We ourselves have seen three instances in which the Shark was led by the Pilot. When the Shark neared the ship the Pilot swam close to the snout, or near one of the pectoral fins of the animal. Sometimes he darted rapidly forwards or sidewards as if looking for something, and constantly went back again to the Shark. When we threw overboard a piece of bacon fastened on a great hook, the Shark was about twenty paces from the ship. With the quickness of lightning the Pilot came up, smelt at the dainty, and instantly swam back again to the Shark, swimming many times round his snout and splashing, as if to give him exact information as to the bacon. The Shark now began to put himself in motion, the Pilot showing him the way, and in a moment he was fast upon the hook.'

This pilot fish is, of course, not to be confused with the remora, or shark sucker, *Echeneis*, a fish on whose head there is a disk aptly described as 'like the corrugated rubber on the sole of a sand shoe.' With this disk it attaches itself to the body of a shark, thereby travelling at ease and, no doubt, finding plenty of 'leavings' from its host. So strong is the instinct for attachment that in an aquarium the fish will fasten itself to the glass window of its tank. In the Torres Straits and other tropical waters the natives when catching turtle make good use of this propensity. A string is tied to the remora's tail and the fish thrown in the direction of the sighted turtle. It soon makes fast to the quarry and both are then hauled in. Legends of the power of this fish to delay ships are numerous, many of them going back to

classical times.   Pliny tells us: 'Winds may blow and storms
may rage, yet the echeneis controls their fury, restrains their
mighty force, and bids ships stand still in their career. . . .
Alas for human vanity when the prows of ships, beaked as
they are with brass and iron and armed for battle, can be
arrested and riveted to one spot by a little fish, no more than
some half-a-foot in length.   At the battle of Actium, it is
said, a fish of this kind stopped the praetorian ship of
Antonius in its course at the moment when he was hastening
from ship to ship to encourage and exhort his men, and so
compelled him to leave it and go on board another.   Hence
it was that the fleet of Caesar gained the advantage in the
onset and charged with a redoubled impetuosity.   In our
own time, too, one of these fishes arrested the ship of the
Emperor Caius (Caligula) in its course when he was returning
from Astura to Antium, and thus, as it proved, did an in-
significant fish give presage of great events, for no sooner
had the emperor returned to Rome than he was pierced by
the weapons of his own soldiers.'   He goes on to say that
when it was perceived that the emperor's galley was the only
one not making progress some of the sailors in that galley
immediately jumped into the sea and, searching along the
ship's side, found an echeneis holding fast to the rudder.

But on this subject, as on many others, we must not take
Pliny too seriously.   As commentators have observed, both
stories are complete fabrications by contemporaries of the
heroes mentioned.   The first was no doubt invented to
palliate the disgrace of Antony's defeat; the second probably
records a ruse on the part of Caligula's crew to obtain relief
from excessive exertion.

Higher in the scale, on land, instances of this same com-
mensalism may be seen in the relationship between some of
the natives of Africa and the honey-bird.   Richard St. Barbe
Baker, in his *Men of the Trees*, writes: 'I have seen a honey-bird
lead a hunter to a hollow tree in which there is honey ready
to be taken.'   He then describes how one of these birds
came up close to his native hunter, 'perched in the bough
of a nearby tree and started chirping noisily.'   Having got

the native's attention 'it flitted from bough to bough in the direction of the hollow tree, returning every now and again and perching quite close to the lad, as if to make quite sure that he was following.' Eventually they reached the denser part of the forest, away from the game track, and high up in a tall tree they could see a hole, in and out of which bees were flashing. Taking a piece of lighted wood and some tinder with him, the native climbed the tree, smoked the bees, and came down again with a supply of honey. All this time the bird had been waiting patiently, and now it was rewarded with a liberal supply of grubs in the comb.

Similar accounts of this mutual assistance come from Rhodesia and from the Lango and Thonga tribes. While on the subject of bees it may be interesting to note that our expression 'honeymoon' possibly arose from the old Teuton custom of drinking mead for thirty days after every wedding.

Sometimes when under the water I would see droves of small blue jelly-fish pulsating their way along, calm and dignified, utterly unconscious of the thousands of their own species which, cast on the shore with every tide, shine in the sun like disks of burnished silver. At other times there would pass one or more of the little grey medusae, whose upper surface of lace-like filaments forms a richer rosette than any functionary's badge of office. There did not seem to be any of the larger cyanea, common in Bermuda, whose clammy jelly wraps itself round the body like a poultice and whose stinging cells can leave their mark and their memory for many days. Even when dry these cells can cause irritation to the human throat and nose. Dr. Muir Evans, in his book *Sting-fish and Seafarer*, tells how after the summer herring season off the east coast of England the nets are overhauled in preparation for the autumn fishing. Should the nets have been shot, as they often are, when the sea is full of jelly-fish, the dried bodies of these 'jellies' will have so impregnated the nets with their venom that an epidemic showing symptoms akin to asthma may break out among the girls who are mending the nets.

The fish in the Red Sea were rather more elusive than

elsewhere, though I understand that they are in greater evidence in summer, when the water is warmer; nevertheless, I moved among clouds of mauve and silver midgets who hovered and darted about the coral like specks of dust in a

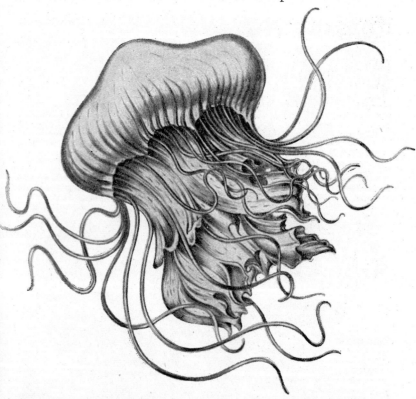

sunbeam or humming birds on the edge of a tropical forest. Pairs of golden chaetodonts would pursue their daily routine irrespective of my presence, and sometimes one of the larger surgeon fish would glide from one cranny to another, showing his yellow pectoral fins against the deep ultramarine of his body.

It was strange how the 'atmosphere' in the water varied from day to day. Sometimes it was as exhilarating as an April day in England; at other times, though rarely, it could be more like February with an east wind. It was on one of these latter occasions that I visited an outlying clump of porites. This species is one of the most important reef-building corals in the Pacific, growing up into great solid masses of rock, but in the Red Sea it only appears occasionally. This particular piece rose from the sandy sea-floor with an

isolated grandeur. Looking down from above, one could see that it was indented and fissured, but when I got to the bottom I found that in addition to these crevices it was deeply under-cut. What was much more important to me just then, there lurked, in the shadows of the overhanging ledges, rock-fish three and four feet in length. With stealthy movements

they circled the base of that rock. Again and again they
went round, each time eyeing me with far too great an
interest. I couldn't help remembering that on the Barrier
Reef of Australia and among the South Sea Islands these

fish can be terribly sudden in their attack. They are more
feared than sharks by the pearl-divers. Instances have been
known where they have stalked a diver for a whole day before
coming in for their pound of flesh.

There had been several days of strong wind and consequent
rough sea, so that the water was murky from the stirred-up

G

sand; furthermore, out here by this isolated monolith the temperature of the water was considerably lower than usual. The atmosphere was definitely non-conducive to aesthetic contemplation. After a short stay below, I returned to the launch.

Other days in other places the sun seemed to shine through the water with all the exaltation that accompanies it on shore. At times one seemed to be living within, or on the other side of, a Chinese painting. Like those delicately drawn trees and temples and birds and people who fade into tenuous mists, so the fish and the branching corals seemed to hang suspended as if on a tinted canvas.

Although most of the hard corals expand only at night, there was no suggestion of suspended animation during the day; indeed, everything seemed to be as actively alive as a hive of bees or a nest of ants. But there was none of that hurry and bustle that is such a feature of terrestrial life. A wonderful serenity of purpose pervaded everything, from the mottled skate lying tranquil by the edge of the reef, or the clams with their mantles picked out in divers colours, to the gorgeous little nudibranchs or sea slugs who crept over the rocks, exhibiting colours as bright as any national standard.

But over and above the unending kaleidoscope of interest which presents itself to any diver, there must always be the added attraction that during the time below it is possible to forget the power of gravity. It is like being in a world of dreams where we can fly or float at will, and there is none of that everlasting effort necessary to support our weight. Should we wish to explore a chasm which may yawn before us, we have only to cast ourselves forward and, lo and behold, even with a hundredweight of ballast attached to us we *float* into the depths. No eagle's feather ever dropped more lightly on the desert sand than our feet on the bottom of the pool, and should there be any trouble about returning, we merely unhook our waist-belt of chain and let it fall, whereupon we shoot to the surface. It is not, however, all clean sand and coral, neither is it always inviting. Wide areas of fine mud exist in which little grows but eel grass. This is the home

of the sea-horse, who twines his tail so caressingly about the
plants, of the little trunk fish or sea-cow, of numerous pipe
fish and trigger fish allied to those we have already met in the
sargassum weed, and of the shrimp fish. This last has, for

mouth, a long tube through which it sucks its nourishment from the mud and, the better to perform this function, it has acquired the habit of swimming in a vertical position. Not only that, but its tail has gradually bent out of the straight, so that it now comes out of the abdomen, while the dorsal fin having moved astern carries on the line of the body. Thus, standing on its head and propelled, spine first, by the fins which have congregated along its ventral surface, it moves and has its being.

Sand, whether rippled by wind or water, takes the same forms; traceries of miniature dunes, seemingly parallel, get interwoven in endless variations. In one case silver dust fanned by the lightest airs, in the other a heavy conglomerate moulded by tons of water. I sometimes wonder if it isn't the same with most of us. Whatever the circumstances, whatever the guiding force, mightn't the pattern of our lives have been the same? We like to think differently, but are we right?

A characteristic of the sea-floor which impressed me when diving was its cleanness. There was nothing dead to be seen, nothing putrefying. Except for clean and empty shells, there was no more sign of dissolution than one sees on land. People in Britain are sometimes heard to remark: 'Strange that one never sees a dead donkey'; people in India say: 'Strange that one never sees a dead elephant.' But what dead animals does one see? How often does one see a dead animal of any kind in England? Except after a sudden crisis of cold, how often does one see even a dead bird? Under water, as on land, scavengers abound. Crabs, lobsters, burrowing worms, and many other mundifying forms of marine life are as ubiquitous and eager as their counterparts on dry land. I was reminded of this while revising this book. It was on a day in mid June, two days after I had thrown a dead mouse on to the grass outside my cottage in Wales. I had hoped that the tawny owl that lives in the larch-trees would have found it, forgetting that in all probability owls only like the food that they themselves have killed. The mouse was still there forty-eight hours later. The weather being warm I thought to move the corpse a little farther from the house, but, when I went to do so, I noticed that a small lump of soil lay over it, as if knocked there by a sheep. On closer examination I found that it was adhering to the fur. Then, as I pondered for a moment, I saw the mouse move. It was hardly more than a quiver, but it was quite definite. It happened again, and again. Each time a slight jerk forward. So I watched, and, as I did so, I could see that something was at work in the grass close to the mouse's head. The grasses were being stirred. And every few moments there would be that slight twitch to the body. Carefully bending a few grasses to one side, I caught a glimpse of a black-and-yellow beetle, cross-striped and brilliant as a wasp. I left the scene of action then for a few hours. When I returned, the mouse's head had disappeared underground. Next day the body was almost entirely out of sight. The following day only the end of the tail was visible. The day after that the tail had gone too, and loose earth covered the spot where the mouse had lain. I did nothing then for three days, but on the fourth morning I opened the ground with a spade. At a depth of five inches I found the mouse. All its hair had been removed and mixed with the loose earth of excavation which now filled the burrow through which the mouse had been drawn. Beside the body were two of the black-and-yellow beetles. Presumably, either they had already laid their eggs or they were about to do so, near the corpse. Thus their larvae when hatched would have a food supply ensured. Thus another dead animal had been hidden.

CHAPTER XII

CAMOUFLAGE

ONE of the greatest surprises when under water was the inconspicuousness of the 'conspicuous' fish. We are accustomed to think of coral fish as brightly coloured, and so they are; we are accustomed to think of them as bizarre in pattern, and so they are; but in most cases neither of these qualities is particularly apparent in their own surroundings. In the shallow water of an aquarium against an unnatural background the fish show up vividly, but with a dozen or twenty feet of water over them, instead of as many inches, the colours take on the mellowness of an old master rather than the crudity of a new one, and the fish are no more obvious than a green-headed mallard among reeds, or a butterfly at rest in a garden.

Among birds there can be few more gorgeous than the peacock, and few who can be more conspicuous when strutting on the castle lawn, yet here is how Abbot H. Thayer describes this bird when seen in its forest home: 'From the golden-green of the forest's sunlight, through all its tints of violet-glossed leaves in shadow, and its coppery glimpses of sunlit bark or earth, all imaginable forest-tones are to be found in this bird's costume; and they "melt" him into the scene to a degree past all human analysis.

'Up in the trees, seen from below, his neck is at its bluest, and when sunlit, perfectly represents blue sky seen through the leaves. Looked *down* on, in the bottom shades of the jungle, it has rich green sheens which "melt" into the surrounding foliage. His back, in all lights, represents golden-green foliage, and his wings picture tree-bark, rock, etc., in sunlight and in shadow. His green-blue head is equipped with a crest which greatly helps it against revealing its contour when it moves. Accompanying its every motion, this crest is, as it were, a bit of background moving with it. The bare white cheek-patch, on the other hand, "cuts a hole," like a lighted foliage-vista, in the bird's face. The tail, when

spread or even when shut, "mingles" in a thousand ways
with its jungle surroundings.   The ocelli, guaranteed by their
forest-scenery colours to vanish into the *background* at a short

distance, have one peculiarly fantastic use. Smallest and
dimmest near the body, and growing bigger and *brighter* in
even progression towards the circumference of the tail, they
inevitably lead the eye away from the bird, till it finds itself
straying amid the foliage beyond the tail's evanescent border.'

It is the same with fish and most other brightly coloured creatures in nature, though there are, of course, individuals such as the caterpillar of the magpie moth, the brimstone butterfly, and the nudibranchs mentioned in the last chapter, whose characteristic markings or colours do not disguise them but are recognized by their enemies as significant of an unpleasant taste, thereby achieving for their owners an immunity from attack, or, as in the extreme case mentioned in Chapter II, an escape from the kitchen via the hands of an artist!

W. J. Crozier states that one of the brightly coloured Bermudian nudibranchs, when irritated or attacked, excretes from the edges of its mantle a bluish-white substance, unpleasant to fishes and various marine invertebrates, and that in addition to this it has at all times a disagreeable and penetrating odour which causes fish who come near it to retreat quickly without touching it. Other creatures, like the wasp and the skunk, flaunt their livery in the knowledge that their powers of offence are known to all, but, apart from these few arrogant beings, there is a mighty host of others who use their decoration in more modest manner. It seems, at first thought, impossible that emerald-green fish should find adequate cover among the petals of pink coral, but then emerald green is the complementary colour of that particular shade of pink, and the fish are thereby absorbed into its shadows. It seems impossible that blue fish should be lost amid clusters of cream coral, but in southern Europe the sun on the yellow buildings throws blue shadows, and, here, we are thinking of latitudes far nearer the equator than even Palermo.

Another aspect of this blue coloration is mentioned by W. H. Longley. Writing of the coral reef fish in the Tortugas Islands, he says: 'Among the Tortugas fishes the lighter blues at least are correlated with the habit of swimming habitually well above the bottom in water of moderate depth. These tints are peculiarly inconspicuous in the eyes of an observer at a lower level, and photographs of fishes banded with other colours show that the effect of the blue is to blot out its possessor's contour under that condition, since at a distance of a few feet the blue gray elements in patterns are indistinguishable from the colour of the watery background.' This correlation of markings with habit almost certainly applies to other colours also.

There is a fish very common in Tahiti whose black and white bands and flowing dorsal fin command immediate attention when it is taken from the water, though it is hard to see when swimming in its natural element. As it moves, with

every now and then a quick change of axis not unlike that of a flat stone or coin when dropped into water, the black and white bands appear as annular or semicircular patterns almost identical with the flicker of light on the surface. To add to the illusion, the long filamentous development of the upper fin blends in as the crisp edge of a wavelet. That is, of course, only a defence from above, and I have not seen this fish when diving, but if ever I want to re-create for myself a vision of the strange flickering light which penetrates those waters I think of the movements of this fish, just as when I want to visualize those same movements I remember the fluttering light transmitted through the scalloped surface of the lagoon.

Besides the fish who seldom move far from their own particular crevice and who dodge into that shelter at the least approach of danger, we have others who prefer to remain immobile and trust to their protective patterns for salvation. There is one, some three inches in length, and

marked like a zebra with clear-cut vertical bars of black and
white, who can be as inconspicuous among the intersecting
branches of white stagshorn coral as our own cock pheasants
can be when lying close under a spray of bracken.   Others,

again, depend for their safety on markings whose chief function appears to be disguise of the silhouette.   The 'rock
beauty,' found all over the West Indies and north as far as
Bermuda, has its body divided vertically into three portions,
of which the first and last are pure gold, and the middle one
ebony black; a relation of his in the Pacific is divided into

three horizontal zones of black and silver white. Others depend on dark splodges on a light skin, or light splodges on a dark skin, to break up the continuity of their form. It is interesting to note that the native warriors of the Marquesas Islands, with whom Herman Melville was a prisoner, tattooed their faces with similar broad bands and circular patches, taking hints no doubt from what they saw in the water, and finding these patterns the most effective disguise for their features among the strong lights and shades of tropical vegetation. As a parallel, which gives weight to this idea, we are told that in the Ellice Islands, farther to the west, if an untattooed native presumed to any of the privileges of one who was fully ornamented, he was quickly rebuked with the remark: 'You are not like a highly coloured fish.'

One day in Bermuda, when swimming in shallow water over clear sand, I noticed a number of black spots moving in the water. They seemed no bigger than pennies, and yet they darted here, there, and everywhere. It was only by the closest observation that I realized they were the ocelli on the tail of a silver fish which frequents those shores, so perfectly did their owners take on the colour of the water or reflect the sand over which they moved.

This reflection must be one of the greatest aids to concealment in forms of aquatic life which are constantly moving from place to place. Time and again I have watched fish like the white grunt and the porgy, both of which would, normally, be considered silvery white, and as they passed by coral, rock, or weed their scales reflected the colours of their surroundings to such an extent as to render them almost invisible. We can imagine, too, how our own freshwater fish like the roach or tench can lie motionless among the reeds, reflecting the stems and leaves, and so achieving almost as great an obliteration of their bodies as those portions of the walls of our houses on which we hang mirrors.

Another point is that many seaweeds have a polished surface, and just as the high lights reflected from a motor-car may be almost any colour except that of the car itself, so the variegated serpentining weeds may throw back coloured lights and shades against which the gayest fish may lurk unseen. There is also the capability of actual change of colour which seems to be a property of nearly all marine life. Most of us can remember our early disappointments when, having caught a richly coloured rockfish and put him for safe keeping in a shallow pool, we found later that he had turned as dull in hue as the rock over which he lay.

My observations under water seemed to indicate that, even apart from their background, there is among many species a constant varying of colour. Shoals of blue-striped grunts, when passing, had their fins and tail any shade from gold to deep brown; if resting for a moment, their sides became suffused with dark vertical bands. The blue angel can appear in any dress from pale cerulean to deep cobalt blue, accentuating or diminishing at will. A red hind, stealthy as a cat, stalked my white shoes to within a few inches, its colour changing from red to pale yellow, with momentary appearances of vertical white bands.

On the Barrier Reef of Australia there is a prawn that has the power of forming blue, red, or yellow pigments, and, by altering their proportions, of producing any colour, or colours, that it wishes. Furthermore, it can develop the pigment in horizontal or longitudinal stripes at will, so that a colour scheme to match almost any background can be produced.

The colours of most fish are not composed of pigment. They are structural, that is to say they are due to the refraction of light as in a precious stone, or as in a peacock's feather, which changes its hues with the varying angles of the incidence of light. An ever-surprising example of the same effect occurs in the age-old fossils of butterflies' wings where, with perfect reproduction of the surface texture, the clay exhibits all the colours of the original insect. Death quickly alters the structure of a fish's skin, hence the evanescence of its colouring. I once saw an octopus dying, on the beach at Tahiti. It had been purple in the water, to match the coral where it lay. But once on shore wave after wave of varying iridescent colours suffused its body. With every

nervous spasm a fresh kaleidoscopic change surged from tentacle to tentacle.   Yet when the animal was dead it showed
nothing brighter than one sees on a dead haddock.

Longley states that 'not only do fishes change their colour

and shade, but some have two or more alternative systems of
markings in which their colours may appear,' and he goes
on to say: 'One may almost dare state it as a law, that when
any species has alternative patterns of longitudinal stripes (or
self-colour) and transverse bands, the former is shown when
the fish that displays it is in motion, while the latter tends

strongly to appear whenever it comes to rest,' and he adds a note: 'Since this was written it has been observed that like many fishes the squid when at rest in the water is transversely banded but replaces these bands by longitudinal stripes when it begins to move.'

We had squids under observation at Ghardaqa, and though their powers of running through the chromatic scale were a constant interest, their powers of perception were even more surprising. On one occasion I watched a specimen swimming close to the jetty in a few feet of water. With gentle movements of his fins he passed along, apparently unseeing or heedless of the humans who were hardly more than a dozen feet away. In his eight shorter tentacles he held a fish, on which he was slowly feeding, while the remaining two arms, longer than the others, waved and groped about as if seeking further plunder. Two natives entered the water some twenty yards away, hoping to surround him with a net, but no sooner had their feet touched the surface than the creature, with powerful belchings of the water in its body cavity, shot straight out to sea and was lost to view.

Most of the fish that we brought into the aquarium varied from moment to moment according to the background that we gave them. Perhaps the most interesting discovery concerned a parrot fish who did not change his actual colours at all, but whose colours appeared entirely different according to the light in which he was seen. When the light was behind the observer the fish was a strong blue and purple, but when the light was behind the fish the portions that had been purple showed as yellow, this change being due to the fins acting as a filter of light and only allowing the yellow rays of the sun to pass through, at the same time reflecting the complementary purple ones.

R. W. Shufeldt, writing in *The American Naturalist* on the psychology of fishes, says: 'The Snowy Grouper, when over-teased in any way, or sometimes without even that provocation, or when its food is presented to it, whether the act be voluntary or involuntary, passed through a peculiar fit or spasm, simulating all the symptoms of a dying fish. Not only this, but the specimen so behaving *changes in colour* from the normal brownish-black to a pale leaden hue, and as the spasmodic stage of the attack subsides, the fish comes to lie perfectly motionless upon its side, or else floats on the bottom, belly upwards. It will remain in this condition for nearly half an hour, when signs of animation again make their appearance, and the individual gradually assumes its former normal condition and colour. The Big-Eye is another species exhibiting somewhat similar attacks under nearly like conditions, but this species, I am told, sometimes dies in one of its more violent spasms. It is a well-known fact that some species of large fishes that prey upon smaller species will not devour them unless captured when making an exciting attempt to escape, and in full vigour of health. They will not touch a dead specimen, or even one in the act of dying. . . . Now, this peculiar fit that seizes the young of the Snowy Grouper may be due to the result of an acute reaction caused by fear; but, on the other hand, it may be something of the nature of "feigning death," and thus be useful to the form in nature. Possibly there may be some large form in the seas that preys upon young Snowy Groupers, and *prefers* to take them only in the excitement of actual chase, and ignores a dead or dying one.'

An amusing instance of a similar though entirely uncontrolled power of colour change in human beings is told by Apsley Cherry-Garrard in his story of Scott's last expedition to the south pole. There he relates how from living amid snow and ice the eyes of one member of the expedition changed from brown to blue, and that under the same conditions his own beard, which would normally have been brown, came out white.

But the subject is inexhaustible. Instances on the reef could be multiplied to fill a book; even *Mussa fragilis*, the lowly rose coral, when brought into the aquarium was seen to alter its tone to match its new surroundings.

CHAPTER XIII

DROWNED VALLEYS

Across the sea beyond the pearl-tinted island of Shadwan lay the slopes of Sinai. Behind us, to the west, rose a line of granite peaks five, six, and seven thousand feet high. At a casual glance one would have said that they were scarcely an hour's march from the camp, so clearly did the foot-hills rise from the plain, yet, even as the vulture flies, it must be fifteen or twenty miles before it can come to rest on those slopes. The shore for half a mile inland was a raised coral beach. We were, in fact, living on a reef which at some remote period of time had been lifted above the level of the sea. All along that Egyptian coast a mighty upheaval in the earth's crust had taken place, so that now, for a distance of half a mile or more inshore, the land was nothing but sand, dead corals, and shells.

Cross-section of fragment of coral picked up half a mile inshore. Reproduced direct from the coral itself. Approximate age, 50,000 years.

It wasn't a case of searching for any of these. One had only to bend down, as at Towila, to pick up such relics. Though scientists guess their age to be anywhere in the region of fifty to a hundred thousand years, the shells were as perfectly preserved as many we find on our beaches to-day, and the specimens of coral, though broken, were sharp and clean to the touch, and, even for a layman, easily placed alongside the same species collected on the reefs to-day. Fifty to a hundred thousand years may seem a long time, yet we are told, too, that the chaetodonts and other gay fish of the

coral reefs existed in European seas about fifty million
years ago.

Wandering up the dry watercourses of the desert one saw,
on either side, wind-swept slopes from which protruded
patches of these shells. In one place it might be the trumpet
variety; in the next it might be cockles, or sea-urchins, or
oysters. Each species appeared to have been gathered together
in colonies at that momentous hour when the last trickle of
sea-water had drained away, wiping out acres of radiant reef,
and leaving them as bare of life as the town of St. Pierre,
in Martinique, after Mont Pelé had, in 1902, cast forth its
mantle of death.

Equally significant were many of the stones standing half
buried in the sand. Once molten pebbles hurled from volcanic depths, they had lain exposed for thousands of years,
suffering the burning heat of days and the chill of nights,
until at last the inner stresses, carried since their birth, had
split them apart. Now they stood not as single stones, but
as parallel slabs with each surface the exact counterpart of
that which faced it, and each group only needing some
cohesive force to reunite it in every detail. Among the
mountains there seemed no limit to the size of these stones,
and it was awe-inspiring to realize that from time immemorial
these mammoth boulders had stood there unmoved. Even
now internal and external forces are at work, and one day,
perhaps to-morrow, or maybe in ten thousand years, they
will fall in pieces with resounding crashes, and so reach one
stage farther in their journey to the sea.

The mountains themselves rose sheer from the sand which
lay, smooth and flat, caressing each slope and winding its
way higher into the ravines, slowly and steadily smothering
the very parents from which it was born. One mighty rock
stands guard at the entry to the Qena Pass, a huge Plutonic
cone of molten forms, layer after layer arrested in their downward flow. No blade of herbage grows on its sides, nor does
a single seed find welcome on the slopes beyond. Here and
there among the stones and sand of the valley grow thorn
bushes, and drifts of sparse silvery grass which, blown by

H

the wind and glistening in the sun, seem, at a distance, like
the smoke of straggling fires. Once in twenty miles an
orchid seed will find shelter under a stone and, taking root,
will bloom and flourish.

Writing of desert sand dunes, in his book *The Physics of
Blown Sand and Desert Dunes*, Brigadier R. A. Bagnold, F.R.S.,
says: 'Instead of finding chaos and disorder, the observer
never fails to be amazed at a simplicity of form, an exactitude
of repetition and a geometric order unknown in nature on
a scale larger than that of crystalline structure. In places
vast accumulations of sand weighing millions of tons move
inexorably, in regular formation, over the surface of the
country, growing, retaining their shape, even breeding, in a
manner which, by its grotesque imitation of life, is vaguely
disturbing to an imaginative mind. Elsewhere the dunes are
cut to another pattern—lined up in parallel ranges, peak
following peak in regular succession like the teeth of a
monstrous saw for scores, even hundreds of miles, without
a break and without a change of direction, over a landscape
so flat that their formation cannot be influenced by any local

geographical features. Or again we find smaller forms, rare among the coastal sand hills, consisting of rows of coarse-grained ridges even more regular than the dunes. Over large areas of accumulated sand the loose, dry, uncemented grains are so firmly packed that a loaded lorry driven across the surface makes tracks less than an inch in depth. Then, without the slightest visual indication of a change, the sub-stance only a few inches ahead is found to be a dry quicksand through which no vehicle can force its way. At times, especially on a still evening after a windy day, the dunes emit, suddenly, spontaneously, and for many minutes, a low-pitched sound so penetrating that normal speech can be heard only with difficulty.'

Inside the pass, peaks rise up. On the one side granite, sharp and crystalline in form, rose, crimson, and lavender in colour. On the other side turbulent slag-heaps of gargantuan size, broken black basalt, as if cast up from Vulcan's own kitchen. Afar, beyond the porphyry mines once worked by the Romans, the road stretches again across the desert towards the setting sun, towards the Nile, towards Luxor, and towards the glory that was Egypt.

When the time came to leave Ghardaqa I asked Dr. Cross-land how best to show my appreciation of the sailors and others, without whose help my journey would have been in vain. He suggested that the present of a sheep would meet the case, explaining that it would be divided in traditional portions. This, then, was agreed upon, and my last memory of the camp is of a black, bob-tailed sheep being led in by three bedouins who, on arrival, sat down and waited for our ambassadors to come and parley with them.

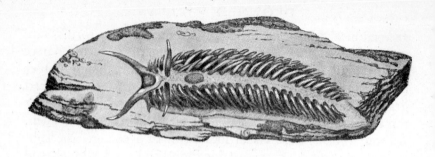

CHAPTER XIV

HOME WATERS

THE fauna and flora of the tropic seas are luxuriant almost to profligacy. Compared with what is to be found in those waters anything that we see in our own cooler latitudes must seem meagre, almost stunted. Yet there is a wealth of interest to be found at home even between the tide levels of our shores or in the shallow sea. At high tide, when the rocks and sandy beaches are covered, opportunities for observation may not be so plentiful, but, as each tide recedes, zone after zone is laid bare, each with its characteristic colonies or individuals of animal and vegetable life. In the pools above high-water mark, where only the splash of breaking waves supplies the necessary minimum of salt, there are animals that cannot live in undiluted sea-water. At the other extreme, near to the range of lowest tide-marks, there are animals that cannot long survive in air. And between those limits there are many hundreds of species whose way of life, in sand or mud or on rock, is adapted to the long or short alternate periods of complete exposure or immersion occasioned by the tides.

The nature of a rock and its situation determine the forms of life living on it. In soft rock we find burrowing animals, molluscs and worms, as well as many others, small crabs, fish, etc., who though not borers themselves are glad to make use of the excavations which in time have become deserted by their owners; whereas on hard rock it will be encrusting forms such as the sponges. On wild headlands, buffeted ceaselessly by heavy waves, there may be no more than a few limpets, whose outer form is shock-resisting, yet within the shelter of a bay the same variety of rock may be covered with a richly varied fauna.

The nature, too, of mud or sand will determine its occupants, as, for example, in a tidal estuary where the animals that thrive will, of necessity, be those which can endure both salt and fresh water. Where there is comparatively coarse sand the amount of organic debris available as food is unlikely to be as much as in a finer silt, and this is bound to affect the density of its population. In mud special adaptations for breathing may be necessary, and these again impose restrictions.

The most remunerative time for search is when the tide is low, particularly at the period of the spring or autumn equinox when the extremes of high and low water are at their greatest, owing to the united rather than the opposing pull of the sun and moon. Under the garlands and tassels of weed, among the stones, under the boulders, and in the pools there are anemones of almost every colour, there are starfish of unexpected shapes, there are sea-slugs, there are crabs with claws adapted for swimming, and lobsters with abbreviated tails (to our way of thinking), and, of course, hosts of shells, each with its living occupant.

For the most part on bare sand there is little to be seen suggesting life except innumerable worm-casts, with, not very far from each, small depressions. Beneath or between any of these there is a worm or a shell-fish in hiding, waiting for the tide to return. As but one example of how thickly a species can be distributed, it has been estimated that on some of the Scottish beaches a thousand or more of the little white bivalve known as *Tellina tenuis* may exist below the surface of one square yard. Worms can be there, too, in similar quantities. Starfishes and varieties of the sea-urchin may also be present.

The common cockle likes to lie an inch or two below the surface of the sand. It has but slight power of movement. On the other hand the common razor-shell buries itself to a depth of a foot or more and can go deeper with great rapidity. Sometimes at extreme low water a man may be seen walking backwards by the water's edge. He carries with him a thin iron bar with which every now and again he probes the sand. Each time that he does so he brings forth one of these razor-shells clasping the rod firmly between its valves. As thrushes discover worms in garden lawns and as gulls reap their own particular harvest by stamping on mud, so also man induces this mollusc to betray its presence. Sensing the footfalls overhead it retreats, squirting out the surplus water from its body as it does so. In Scotland it is known as the spout-fish.

The anemones may be of almost any colour. In addition to the more common red and green varieties there will be found others, beige, dove grey, old gold, silver white. Some have viridian tentacles tipped with purple, others have a translucent crest shining like quartz crystals. The great dahlia anemones are there too, big flowers four, five, and six inches across, all shades of crimson and rose, their bodies striped and spotted, their tentacles barred; rich in form and colour as anything in the tropics.

The starfishes may be of the familiar five-rayed stellate forms, grey or reddish brown in colour, but they may also be of less usual shape and colour. There are the scarlet cushion-stars with bodies thick, as if padded, and arms so short that the whole outline is almost a pentagon. There are the sun-stars, crimson and gold, with arms varying in number from eight to thirteen. From a boat, in shallow water, may be seen stars of deepest Tyrian purple, or the bird's-foot star whose arms seem only differentiated from its thin paper-like body by their scarlet colour.

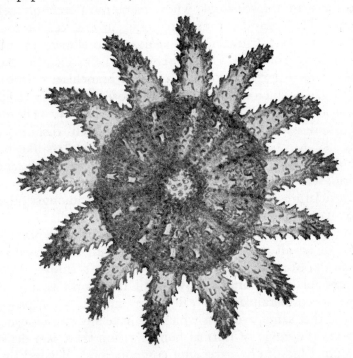

Starfish are carnivorous, feeding on molluscs, worms, crustacea, etc. For this reason they can do a great deal of harm to the plaice fisheries, for the plaice feed on the same shell-fish. It has been calculated that in one area near Plymouth the annual destruction wrought by starfish on the molluscs amounts to the same as that consumed by the annual human catch of plaice. Partly for that reason but also because of the nuisance caused by their entanglement in nets, fishermen have been in the habit of 'killing' them by chopping them in two before throwing them overboard. Far from achieving its purpose, this action has an exactly contrary effect, for the starfish can not only renew a lost limb, as many of the crustacea can also do, but can regenerate a whole body from the fragments of one thus divided. Each fragment therefore becomes in time a new individual and wreaks its vengeance, 'hydra-headed,' on its persecutor.

Perhaps the loveliest of the less known forms of life on the shore are the sea-slugs, whose name most certainly belies them. They may be found in pools, in crevices of rocks, or under stones, grazing on sponges, corallines, or weed as brightly coloured as themselves. Their scientific name *nudibranchs* is derived from the external branchiae, or breathing organs, which in the form of plumose papillae, in clusters or in lines, are the chief ornament of their body. The delicacy and variety of these plumes completely disguise the slug-like form so that it often appears as a glass-like fairy creature, whose colours, too, remind one of an unsubstantial world. Even science has relaxed into the poetic in its nomenclature of these individuals, giving us, amongst others, such names as Eolis, Idalia, Fiona, Antiopa, Scyllaea.

But all that I have written in this chapter is mere platitude, born of an all too slight acquaintance with these creatures. In any pool there is interest for a lifetime's study. It is a commonplace to remark how small the world is, but not quite so commonplace to realize how minute is the proportion of that same world of which we have any consciousness. Beyond the range of normal human vision there is a density of animal life utterly exceeding computation. Beyond those senses of which we have consciousness in our own bodies there are in other animals senses of whose functioning we have but the faintest idea. When all is said and done there probably remains, even beyond our wildest dreams, a cosmos as far beyond our powers of apprehension as the theory of relativity is beyond the understanding of a starfish.

POSTSCRIPT

WHEN this book was first contemplated I visualized it as scarcely more than a series of drawings, to be made under water, with accompanying explanatory notes. But, when travelling, incidents happened, both on ship and shore, which seemed to be worth recording, so that eventually the pages covered a wider range. Since the publication of the first edition, in 1938, many items of relevant interest have come my way, and these I have now incorporated in the text. I have also added to the number of illustrations, and because I have been conscious of the limitations of wood-engraving in a book of this kind I have in the new format substituted reproductions of the original drawings.

My thanks are due to Allen Lane, of Penguin Books, who first commissioned the book and by whose consent this enlarged version is published, also to the British Museum and the Victoria and Albert Museum for permission to reproduce the drawings on pages 52 and 36 respectively, and to the Cole Museum of Reading University for a similar courtesy concerning those on pages 57 and 89. I would like, too, to say a special word of thanks to Mr. H. G. Parrack and other members of the firm of Odhams for their care in the reproduction of the drawings.

R. G.

WALTHAM SAINT LAWRENCE, BERKS.,
    1945.

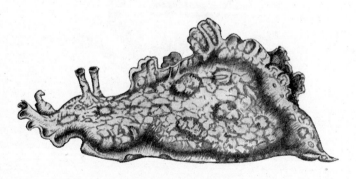

BIBLIOGRAPHY

Nonsuch : Land of Water, by William Beebe.

Field Book of the Shore Fishes of Bermuda, by William Beebe and John Tee-Van.

Desert and Water Gardens of the Red Sea, by Cyril Crossland.

Littoral Fauna of Great Britain, by Nellie B. Eales.

Sting-fish and Seafarer, by H. Muir Evans.

Science of the Sea, edited by G. Herbert Fowler.

Coral Reefs and Atolls, by J. Stanley Gardiner.

An Introduction to the Study of Fishes, by A. C. L. G. Günther.

The Great Barrier Reef of Australia, by W. Saville Kent.

Colour in Nature, by Marion Newbigin.

A History of Fishes, by J. R. Norman.

Giant Fishes, Whales and Dolphins, by J. R. Norman and F. C. Fraser.

Camouflage in Nature, by W. P. Pycraft.

Wonders of the Great Barrier Reef, by T. C. Roughley.

The Seas, by F. S. Russell and C. M. Yonge.

Concealing Coloration in the Animal Kingdom, by Abbot H. Thayer.

Life of the Shore and Shallow Sea, by Douglas P. Wilson.

Coral and Atolls, by F. Wood-Jones.

A Year on the Great Barrier Reef, by C. M. Yonge.